D1372625

4 EASY STEPS TO SUCCESSFUL INVESTING

Jonathan D. Pond

AVON BOOKS NEW YORK

AVON BOOKS
A division of
The Hearst Corporation
1350 Avenue of the Americas
New York, New York 10019

Copyright © 1997 by Jonathan D. Pond
Interior design by Rhea Braunstein
Visit our website at **http://AvonBooks.com**
ISBN: 0-380-97472-X

All rights reserved, which includes the right to reproduce this book or portions thereof in any form whatsoever except as provided by the U.S. Copyright Law. For information address Avon Books.

Library of Congress Cataloging in Publication Data:
Pond, Jonathan D.
   4 easy steps to successful investing / Jonathan D. Pond—1st ed.
      p.   cm.
   Includes index.
   1. Investments. 2. Finance, Personal. I. Title.
HG4521.P57 1997   96-46377
332.6—dc21   CIP

First Avon Books Printing: February 1997

AVON TRADEMARK REG. U.S. PAT. OFF. AND IN OTHER COUNTRIES, MARCA REGIS-
TRADA, HECHO EN U.S.A.

Printed in the U.S.A.

FIRST EDITION

OPM   10 9 8 7 6 5 4 3 2 1

INTRODUCTION

This book shows you how to invest wisely and well—whether you're new to investing or have many years of investing experience, whether you have $1,000 to invest or $1,000,000. A few years ago, I became fed up with the complicated, confusing, and conflicting information that bombarded investors from all sides. So I prepared a small brochure entitled "Four Easy Steps to Successful Investing." I sold it primarily by word of mouth. We received over 60,000 requests for it—and many accolades. One investor wrote: "At last, after years of trying my best, your brochure has shown me how to invest my money sensibly. For the first time in my life, I'm optimistic about my financial furture."

This is an expansion of my brochure. It starts out with a discussion on mutual funds. Part I explains how to put together a well-diversified mutual fund portfolio. (If you're completely new to investing, there's an appendix that will quickly explain how investing works.) In Part II I'll show you how to include individual stocks and bonds in your investments, so you can take advantage of all three worthwhile investment categories: mutual funds, stocks, and bonds. In Part III you'll learn how to manage your investments without having to take a lot of time away from your busy life. Finally, in Part IV, I'll provide useful and straightforward guidance on special investing situations such as investing for college, real estate investing, investing when you're retired, and making the most of your retirement plan choices.

You may think that investing is just too complicated. But in reading the pages that follow you'll find that it doesn't have to be that way. You can—and will—be a successful investor. And investing successfully, more than any other part of your financial life, will put you squarely on the road to financial security.

CONTENTS

PART III
Actively Managing Your Investment Portfolio—
An Hour a Month Can Add Thousands
of Dollars to Your Investments Each Year

PART IV
Special Situations

PART I

Four Easy Steps to Investment Success Using Mutual Funds

CHAPTER 1

---ꭥꭥꭥ---

STEP ONE: Figuring Out How Much to Invest in Stock Funds and How Much to Invest in Bond Funds

My easy steps to successful investing really are easy. Each step requires some thought, but I'm here to help you along the way. Investing successfully is crucial to your financial future, so spend some time now going through the four steps so that you can invest your hard-earned savings well enough to achieve your financial dreams. There is no magic here, just a lot of common sense applied to techniques that have been used by successful investors for centuries.

A lot of people are frightened about investing. They have been led to believe that investing is complicated and the average Joe and Jane are simply incapable of making sensible investment decisions. Well, you'll soon find out how straightforward successful investing will be. It won't take long.

To make life a little easier, I'm going to introduce the four steps by using mutual funds exclusively. Most investors start out with mutual fund investments, and even experienced investors and investors with large portfolios should make generous use of mutual funds. Once I've introduced the four easy steps to successful investing in the first four chapters, I will then show you in Part II how to fit individual stocks and bonds into your portfolio. But the guidelines that are presented in this and the following chapter apply to all of your investments—mutual funds as well as individual stocks and bonds.

A Simple Calculation   The following step involves a simple calculation that will help you determine your allocation between stocks and bonds—in other words, of the total money you have available to invest how much should be invested in stocks and how much in bonds? These are the two most frequently used investment categories. There are two other categories—short-term investments and real estate, which are discussed in Chapters 17 and 14, respectively—but I'm not including them here for reasons I'll discuss in those chapters. For the time being, we'll stick with stocks and bonds, or at this stage, stock mutual funds and bond mutual funds.

Three different overall investment allocations are presented in the following discussion. The one you select is up to you, depending on how comfortable you are taking risks. There are risks in stocks and bonds, but stocks are the riskier. If you are comfortable with investment risk, then you will probably opt for the aggressive investment allocation. On the other hand, if you are a bit uncomfortable with taking risk, the conservative allocation may be for you. For those who are somewhere in between, like me, there is a moderate investment allocation as well.

Are you unfamiliar with some of the terms I've been using so far, such as *stocks, bonds, mutual funds,* and *risk?* If you are relatively new to investing or want a quick refresher course, Appendix A explains the basics of investing and what the various kinds of investments are and do.

Aggressive Portfolio Allocation

If you are willing to accept risk in your investments in exchange for the possibility of earning high long-term investment returns, here is the formula for calculating an aggressive investment allocation:

> Subtract your age from 120. The resulting amount is the approximate percentage of the money you have available for long-term investment that you should invest in stocks. The rest should be invested in bonds.

> **EXAMPLE:** A forty-year-old investor is quite comfortable with risk and therefore wants an aggressive portfolio allocation. She would, according to the above formula, invest about 80 percent of her money in stock funds (120 − 40 = 80) and the rest, about 20 percent, in bond funds.

Moderate Portfolio Allocation

I'm most comfortable with a moderate portfolio allocation, which still includes a fairly heavy weighting of stocks in the portfolio. To determine a moderate portfolio allocation, use the following formula:

> Subtract your age from 110. The resulting amount is the approximate percentage of the money you have available for long-term investment that you should invest in stocks. The rest should be invested in bonds.

> **EXAMPLE:** A sixty-five-year-old investor wisely realizes that he needs to continue investing for growth as well as income during retirement. He feels a moderate portfolio allocation would fit the bill. According to the above formula, this inves-

tor would put about 45 percent of his money in stock funds (110 − 65 = 45) and the rest, about 55 percent, in bond funds.

Conservative Portfolio Allocation

If you are less comfortable with the ups and downs of the stock market, a conservative portfolio allocation may be your cup of tea. A conservative allocation will still allow for stock funds in your portfolio, which are essential if your portfolio is going to grow over the years, but the proportion of stocks will be somewhat lower than the aggressive and moderate portfolios. To determine a conservative portfolio allocation, use the following formula:

Subtract your age from 100. The resulting amount is the approximate percentage of the money you have available for long-term investment that you should invest in stocks. The rest should be invested in bonds.

EXAMPLE: A fifty-three-year-old investor is a bit skittish about the stock market. She realizes that stocks are crucial to her long-term investment success, but she will feel most comfortable with a conservative portfolio allocation. According to the conservative investment allocation formula, she would invest about 47 percent of her money in stock funds (100 − 53 = 47) and the rest, about 53 percent, in bond funds.

Please Take Note

• If you are new to stock investing or have previously been uncomfortable with stocks, you may be surprised at the high proportion of stocks that would be in your portfolio based on the above formulas. But stocks have pretty consistently been the best long-term investment compared with bonds and short-term investments like Treasury bills. Yes, stocks do decline periodically—sometimes a lot—but as the following table of annual rates of return by decade for various types of investments shows, stocks are clearly the winners. While stocks didn't always outpace other investments, they did beat bonds and Treasury bills over most of the periods surveyed—and usually by a wide margin.

─────────────────── **Table 1–1** ───────────────────

Compound Annual Rates of Return by Decade

	1930s	1940s	1950s	1960s	1970s	1980s	1990–1995
Large company stocks	−0.1%	9.2%	19.4%	7.7%	5.9%	17.5%	13.0%
Small company stocks	1.4	20.7	16.9	15.5	11.5	15.8	15.3
Long-term corporate bonds	6.9	2.7	1.0	1.7	6.2	13.0	11.3
Long-term government bonds	4.9	3.2	−0.1	1.4	5.5	12.6	11.9
Intermediate-term government bonds	4.6	1.8	1.3	3.5	7.0	11.9	9.0
Treasury bills	0.6	0.4	1.9	3.9	6.3	8.9	4.9
Inflation	−2.0	5.4	2.2	2.5	7.4	5.1	3.4

Source: Stock, Bonds, Bills and Inflation 1996 Yearbook, Ibbotson Associates.

- All three investment allocation formulas are based on your age, so as your age increases (alas, there's nothing you or any of us can do about that), you will gradually invest more money in bonds and less in stocks. In fact, the formula will change each year. But that doesn't mean you need to change your investment allocation every year. These formulas should be rough approximations of how you should invest, not rigid standards. The reason the formulas are keyed to your age is that the older you become, the less time you have to make up for investment losses, and yes, there will be times when you suffer losses. So as you age your investment allocation will gradually become more conservative since bonds are a more conservative investment than stocks.

• A special note to retirees: You may find that the above formulas result in a stock allocation percentage that is lower than you think is appropriate. If you are comfortable with a higher percentage of your money in stocks, by all means allocate your portfolio accordingly. These formulas should be viewed by seniors as indicating a minimum percentage of stock funds and stock in an investment portfolio. If you are over seventy, continue to have at least 30 percent of your long-term investment money in stocks because you still need growth investments in your portfolio to help you keep up with inflation throughout your retirement years. Seniors who have investments they don't think they will need during their lifetimes are, in effect, investing for the next generation. In these instances, your investment allocation may reflect not the allocation for, say, a seventy-five-year-old, but rather the allocation that would be appropriate for your forty-five-year-old child if you expect the child to inherit the portfolio. Investing for retirees is important, so I've devoted all of Chapter 19 to it.

• As I mentioned briefly above, there are two other investment categories in addition to stocks and bonds—real estate and short-term investments such as money market funds and savings accounts. Own-it-yourself income-producing **real estate** can certainly play a role in an investment portfolio for those who have the time and patience to be landlords. But limit your real estate investments to no more than 40 percent of your total portfolio, because real estate investors need to own stocks and bonds as well. If you want to participate in real estate but don't want the hassles of being a landlord, consider investing in a mutual fund that specializes in real estate investments. Don't invest in real estate limited partnerships. See Chapter 14 for some suggestions on investing in real estate.

Short-term investments really have no role in a long-term investment portfolio unless you are so uncomfortable with bond funds that you want to use short-term investments as a substitute. But they simply don't pay enough interest to beat inflation over the years. Short-term investments should be used as a temporary parking place for your money while awaiting attractive investment opportunities or if you are going to need the money in a short time—you are planning to buy a home or your child is going to enter college within a few years. See Chapter 17 for a detailed discussion of short-term investments.

Many people think they need to keep a lot of money set aside in low-interest accounts as "an emergency fund." Since mutual funds and most other investments can be sold in a matter of a few days, it doesn't make much sense to keep a lot of money languishing in checking, savings, or money market accounts or Treasury bills. Keep no more than one month's living expenses in short-term investments as an emergency fund. Invest the rest so that it will have a chance to grow over the years.

That about does it for Step One of the four easy steps to successful investing. Before moving on, use the following table to compute your investment allocation target.

Table 1–2

Your Investment Allocation Target

Check one:

_____ Aggressive
_____ Moderate
_____ Conservative

_____ % Stocks
_____ % Bonds
<u>100%</u> Total

CHAPTER 2

---∞---

STEP TWO: Figuring Out How Much to Invest in Each Stock and Bond Mutual Fund Category

Now that you have determined the approximate percentage of your money that should be invested in stocks and the percentage in bonds, step two will show you how to divvy up your stock money and divvy up your bond money among the various types of stock and bond mutual funds.

Unfortunately, successful investing is a bit more complicated than simply putting all of the money you've earmarked for stocks in a single stock fund and all the money you've earmarked for bonds in a single bond fund. There are many different kinds of stocks and bonds, so there are many different kinds of mutual funds that invest in stocks or bonds. But don't be intimidated by variety, because variety begets opportunity to participate in all important and sensible categories of stocks and bonds.

So let's move on to the way you should divide your money among the various mutual fund categories. If you need a brief refresher on what kinds of investments these various fund categories make, refer to the mutual fund glossary at the end of this chapter.

Investing Recommendations by Age

The following tables are my recommended percentage allocations among four stock fund categories and six bond fund categories for each of three age groups of investors. Recall that in Step One, you assigned overall percentages to both stocks and bonds according to the amount of risk you feel comfortable with and your age. In Step Two, the way you allocate your money among the various stock funds and bond funds also considers your age. Three age groups are reflected in the tables that follow: younger, preretirees, and retirees. Don't let the math scare you. I've included an example on pages 14–15.

Younger

If you are of working age but not yet within ten years of retirement, you have a long time for your investments to grow. (I use the term "younger" here because it's flattering to those of us, including me, who are firmly entrenched in middle age.) Even a fifty-year-old will need his money to last another forty or more years, during which time the cost of living may well quadruple. So the emphasis in the stock and bond portfolios is on those investments with the best long-term growth potential. Of course, with growth comes risk. So this is the highest risk of the three investment allocations, which is entirely ap-

---------- **Table 2–1** ----------

Fund Investment Category Allocation for Younger Investors

STOCK MUTUAL FUNDS Percentage allocation of total money you will invest in stock funds		BOND MUTUAL FUNDS Percentage allocation of total money you will invest in bond funds	
Growth	25	Long-term municipal	25
Growth and income	25	Short/intermediate-term municipal	15
Small company	25		
International	25	Long-term U.S. government	20
	100	Short/intermediate-term U.S. government	10
		Long-term corporate	20
		Short/intermediate-term corporate	10
			100

propriate for investors who won't need most of the money
for decades.

Preretirees

This investment allocation is appropriate for investors who
are within ten years of retirement. Note that it is somewhat
more conservative in the percentages assigned to the various
stock and bond categories. The rationale here is that preretirees need to begin getting a bit less aggressive with their investments as they near their retirement years. But the emphasis
should still be on investments that offer inflation-beating
growth.

--- **Table 2–2** ---

Fund Investment Category Allocation for Preretirees

STOCK MUTUAL FUNDS Percentage allocation of total money you will invest in stock funds		BOND MUTUAL FUNDS Percentage allocation of total money you will invest in bond funds	
Growth	20	Long-term municipal	20
Growth and income	40	Short/intermediate-term municipal	20
Small company government 10%	20	Long-term U.S. government	15
International	20	Short/intermediate-term U.S. government	15
	100	Long-term corporate	15
		Short/intermediate-term corporate	15
			100

Retirees

The third recommended way to allocate your various stock and bond investments is for retirees. Here the shift in emphasis favors the more conservative and higher income-producing categories. Nevertheless, there is still sufficient money invested for growth so that retirees can keep up with inflation throughout their retirement years.

Table 2–3

Fund Investment Category Allocation
for Retired Investors

STOCK MUTUAL FUNDS Percentage allocation of total money you will invest in stock funds		BOND MUTUAL FUNDS Percentage allocation of total money you will invest in bond funds	
Growth	15	Long-term municipal	15
Growth and income	55	Short/intermediate- term municipal	25
Small company	15	Long-term U.S. government	10
International	15	Short/intermediate- term U.S. gov- ernment	20
	100	Long-term corporate	10
		Short/intermediate- term corporate	20
			100

EXAMPLE: Phoebe Phinney is a younger investor with $80,000 available to invest. Her overall investment allocation between stocks and bonds, which she determined in Chapter 1, is 75 percent stocks and 25 percent bonds. Now she wants to allocate her investment money among the various stock and bond mutual fund categories. First, she needs to calculate how much in total she should invest in stocks and how much in bonds. Here's how to do it:

Total to be invested in stocks = the total amount available to invest multiplied by the stock allocation percentage expressed as a decimal.

Total to be invested in stocks = $80,000 × .75 = $60,000.

Total to be invested in bonds = the total amount available to invest multiplied by the bond allocation percentage expressed as a decimal.

Total to be invested in bonds = $80,000 × .25 = $20,000.

Once Phoebe knows how much in total to invest in both stocks and bonds, she can then go to the appropriate table to calculate how much to invest in each stock and bond fund category. Since she's a younger investor, she will refer to Table 2–1. Table 2–4 shows how the information in Table 2–1 can be applied to Phoebe's own situation.

Table 2–4

Phoebe Phinney's Fund Investment Allocation

STOCK MUTUAL FUNDS				BOND MUTUAL FUNDS		
	Total amount to invest in stocks	Percent allocation	Amount to invest in category		Total amount to invest in bonds	Percent allocation	Amount to invest in category
Growth	$60,000 ×	25 =	$15,000	Long-term municipal	$20,000 ×	25 =	$5,000
Growth and income	60,000 ×	25 =	15,000	Short/ intermediate-term municipal	20,000 ×	15 =	3,000
Small company	60,000 ×	25 =	15,000	Long-term U.S. government	20,000 ×	20 =	4,000
International	60,000 ×	25 = 100	15,000 $60,000	Short/ intermediate-term U.S. government	20,000 ×	10 =	2,000
				Long-term corporate	20,000 ×	20 =	4,000
				Short/ intermediate-term corporate	20,000 ×	10 = 100	2,000 $20,000

Why Are There So Many Bond Funds?   Six bond funds is a lot, but in order to invest in all three important bond categories—municipal, U.S. government, and corporate, you need at least three. Then you need to invest in two funds within the three categories, each of which invests in bonds of different maturities. I'll explain more about this later, but if you want to find out now, see pages 23–24.

To show you how a portfolio can be put together under the allocations recommended above, I've prepared two illustrations.

─────────────────────── **Table 2–5** ───────────────────────

Sample Mutual Fund Investment Allocation for a Preretiree

Overall investment allocation preference: Aggressive
Amount available for investment: $30,000
Age 53 (9 years from retirement)
Overall allocation in percentages: 67% stocks (120 − 53) and 33% bonds
Overall allocation in dollars: $20,000 in stocks and $10,000 in bonds

STOCK MUTUAL FUNDS			BOND MUTUAL FUNDS		
	Preretiree			Preretiree	
	%	$		%	$
Growth	20	$4,000	Long-term municipal	20	$2,000
Growth and income	40	8,000	Short/intermediate-		
Small company	20	4,000	term municipal	20	2,000
International	20	4,000	Long-term U.S.		
	100	$20,000	government	15	1,500*
			Short/intermediate-term U.S. government	15	1,500*
			Long-term corporate	15	1,500*
			Short/intermediate-term corporate	15	1,500*
				100	$10,000

*If bond funds require more than a $1,500 minimum, follow the sequence for investing in bond funds that appears on pages 17–19.

Table 2–6

Sample Mutual Fund Investment Allocation for a Retiree

Overall investment allocation preference: Moderate
Amount available for investment: $125,000
Age: 70 (retired)
Overall allocation in percentages: 40% stock (110 − 70) and 60% in bonds
Overall allocation in dollars: $50,000 stocks and $75,000 bonds

STOCK MUTUAL FUNDS			**BOND MUTUAL FUNDS**		
	Retiree			Retiree	
	%	$		%	$
Growth	15	$7,500	Long-term municipal	15	$11,000
Growth and income	55	27,500	Short/intermediate-		
Small company	15	7,500	term municipal	25	19,000
International	15	7,500	Long-term U.S.		
	100	$40,000	government	10	7,500
			Short/intermediate-term		
			U.S. government	20	15,000
			Long-term corporate	10	7,500
			Short/intermediate-		
			term corporate	20	15,000
				100	$75,000

Recommendations for More Modest Portfolios

In order to arrange your portfolio so that it includes all of the above-recommended investments you probably need at least $35,000. The reason for this is that most mutual funds require minimum investment balances of $2,000 or more. If you're not at that lofty level, don't despair. Simply follow my recommendations below for investing more modest amounts of money.

- **If you have less than $5,000 to invest.** Select a balanced mutual fund. These funds invest in both stocks and bonds, so you can start with a "balanced" portfolio in a single mutual fund.
- **If you have over $5,000.** Once you have over $5,000 to invest, you can begin to buy individual mutual funds in sequence. As the money you have available to invest increases over time, you simply buy another fund in the next category. The following is a recommended sequence for purchasing mutual funds in individual categories. While you won't be strictly conforming to your investment allocation percentages, by following these sequences, you can be assured of having a reasonably well-balanced portfolio until the time when you have enough money to take full advantage of the fund investment allocation category table that applies to you.

So if you have more than $5,000 to invest in mutual funds, buy them in the following order:

STOCK FUNDS
1. Growth and income fund
2. Small company fund
3. International fund
4. Growth fund

BOND FUNDS
1. Long-term government fund
2. Short- or intermediate-term government bond fund
3. Long-term municipal bond fund
4. Short- or intermediate-term municipal bond fund
5. Long-term corporate bond fund
6. Short- or intermediate-term corporate bond fund

You may be thinking that this is very tricky and mathematically difficult, but it isn't, particularly if you realize that you don't

have to be especially precise in how you allocate your investments so long as you conform roughly to these guidelines.
The key to success in investment allocation is not so much
being precise in the way you allocate your money as it is
in making sure you are participating in different investment
categories so that you will always have some money in categories that are doing well. This approach also allows you to be
free from any anxiety that you are too heavily invested in
categories that may be doing poorly. The challenge to those
who are building their portfolios is deciding how to invest as
the money available for investment increases. That's what the
above guidelines will help you to do, but I know you won't
be convinced that it can be done without a couple of examples.

EXAMPLE 1: Randy Randall has $8,000 sitting in a bank sav-
ings account. He thinks that he has nowhere near enough
money to be able to invest in anything other than a savings
account or CD. Not true! He can most definitely get started
on an investment program, even at the age of fifty-four.
Since he wants to avoid taking a lot of risk, a conservative
overall investment allocation seems to be best (see page 6).
This would result in his having 46 percent in stocks (100 −
54 = 46) and the rest, or 54 percent, in bonds. Therefore,
with the $8,000 he has available to invest, he should allocate
a little less than $4,000 in stocks and a little more than
$4,000 in bonds. It's not necessary to be so precise, so he
will be perfectly okay splitting the money down the middle—$4,000 in stocks and $4,000 in bonds.

The fund company he has selected has a $2,000 mini-
mum investment requirement, so he can buy two stock
funds and two bond funds. According to the list on page
18 that shows the sequence for adding funds to a portfolio, Randy should put $2,000 each into the first two stock
funds on the list—growth and income funds and a small
company fund. On the bond side of his portfolio, he can
also invest $2,000 in each of the first two bond funds on

the list—a long-term government bond fund and a short-
or intermediate-term government bond fund. So Randy is
well on his way to becoming a successful investor, even
with $8,000.

EXAMPLE 2: Alexis Alexander is 28 and has $12,000 to invest.
Up to this point, the money has been languishing in a savings account, but now she has decided to get serious about
investing and feels most comfortable with a moderate overall
investment allocation (see pages 5–6), which would result in
her having 82 percent in stocks (110 − 28 = 82) and 18
percent in bonds. Translating that into dollars results in
about $10,000 in stocks ($12,000 × .82) and the rest, or
$2,000, in bonds.

The number of funds she can purchase with her available money depends on the minimum initial purchase requirements of the fund company or companies she plans
to use. In this instance, Alexis has selected a fund company that has a $2,500 minimum, which means she could
buy all four stock fund categories—growth, growth and
income, small company, and international—in equal pro-
portions but could not yet buy a bond fund since she has
only $2,000 available to invest in bonds versus a $2,500
minimum. Therefore, she should invest the remaining
$2,000 in a money market fund until she has saved an-
other $500, at which time she should buy the first bond
fund category in the above sequence—a long-term government bond fund. Alternatively, she could invest her
bond fund money in a mutual fund that imposes a minimum initial investment requirement of $2,000 or less.
That's one of the advantages of dealing either with more
than one mutual fund company or with a brokerage firm
that has a mutual fund buying service, such as Charles
Schwab & Co. or Fidelity (see page 222). So even though
Alexis has a modest amount of money to invest, she is
still able to assemble a well-diversified portfolio.

Mutual Fund Glossary

Stock Funds

A stock (or equity) mutual fund invests its money in stocks of individual companies, large and small, new and old, here and abroad. There are many different types of stock funds, characterized by the kind of companies in which the fund invests, and by the fund's particular objective. Here are the main categories of stock mutual funds:

Growth Funds   These funds seek capital gains from companies that have the potential for steady growth in profits. Growth funds aim to achieve a rate of growth that beats inflation without taking the risks necessary to achieve occasional spectacular success. A riskier type of stock fund is *aggressive growth funds*. These attempt to achieve very high returns by investing in more speculative stocks, maximizing capital gains income. Since the growth stocks favored by growth funds and aggressive growth funds pay little or no dividends, neither do these funds distribute many, if any, dividends.

Growth and Income Funds   These seek a more balanced stock portfolio that will achieve capital appreciation as well as current income from dividends. These funds are less risky than growth funds, because the dividend may offset at least some of the periodic losses in stock prices. In times of high market volatility—in either an up or down direction—growth and income funds generally don't rise and fall as much as growth funds.

International Funds   These have been attracting investors' attention because foreign stock markets have pretty consistently outperformed the U.S. stock market. Moreover, there are many excellent companies that trade only on foreign stock exchanges. Therefore, international funds provide additional diversification to a portfolio. Most international funds invest throughout the world. Some invest only in one country or region. *Global stock funds,* however, differ only in that they also invest in U.S. securities.

Bond Funds

A bond mutual fund invests its money in bonds of companies or governments that are as varied as those in which stock funds invest. Bond funds tend to be the more conservative growth- and income-producing portion of an investor's portfolio—although bond fund share prices can and do fluctuate in value. Some bond funds even deliver tax-free income to their investors.

U.S. Government Bond Funds   Backed by the full faith and credit of the U.S. government, these offer total protection from bond default, although the value of government bonds will fluctuate with interest rates like all bonds and bond funds. Most government bond funds hold at least some U.S. Treasury securities (whose interest is exempt from state income taxes unless you hold the fund in a retirement account). One variety of government bond fund, *government mortgage funds,* holds mortgage-backed securities such as those issued by the Government National Mortgage Association (GNMA). Holders of GNMA funds receive both interest income and a partial return of principal, which may be reinvested.

Municipal Bond Funds   These provide investors with a means for tax-free income. Since municipal bond fund prices do not appear in the daily papers and are inconvenient for the individual investor to manage, muni bond funds are a useful way to invest in municipal bonds while avoiding these problems. Interest earned from bonds not issued in the investor's own state is fully taxable in her own state, so in order to produce maximum tax-free income, *single state funds* have been developed that hold municipal bonds from only one state. A California resident owning a California muni fund, for example, will avoid state as well as federal taxes on the fund's interest income. Most municipal bond funds invest in higher rated municipal securities. *High-yield municipal bond funds,* however, invest in lower rated municipal bonds (yes, municipal bonds can default), and are appropriate for investors seeking high interest income who are willing to accept higher risk. Incidentally, high-yield municipal bond funds and high-yield corporate bond funds (discussed below) are, in less polite company, called "junk bond funds."

Corporate Bond Funds   As the name so amply suggests, these buy and trade bonds of corporations. There are two categories of corporate bond mutual funds: *Investment-grade corporate bond funds,* which are composed of higher quality corporate bonds and seek high income with limited risk, and *high-yield corporate bond funds,* which invest in lower rated corporate bonds.

BOND FUNDS COME IN DIFFERENT MATURITIES. I'm sorry to complicate matters a bit more, but this is one situation where complexity begets better investment opportunity. Bond mutual funds are not only categorized according to the type of bonds that the fund will invest in as discussed above—municipals, governments, and corporates—but they are also divided according to the approximate length of maturity of the bonds that the manager puts into the portfolio. There are three maturity levels:

Short-Term Bond Funds (also called limited-term bond funds)   These funds invest in bonds with an average maturity of one to four years.

Intermediate-Term Bond Funds   These funds invest primarily in intermediate-term bonds with an average maturity of four to ten years.

Long-Term Bond Funds These funds usually invest primarily in bonds with an average maturity of more than ten years.

As you have probably already noted from the tables in this chapter, I have suggested that you invest your bond money in funds with varying maturities. In other words, some of the money will go into a short- or intermediate-term bond fund and some will go into a long-term bond fund. There is method in my madness, however. One of the most widely accepted strategies for investing in bonds is called "laddering maturities." Rather than putting all of your money into a single maturity bond fund—be it short, intermediate, or long—laddering maturities means investing in mutual funds (or individual bonds for that matter) with a variety of maturities. By owning bonds with different maturities, you somewhat reduce the risk of losing a lot of principal because of a change in interest rates. For example, if you have all of your bond money in long-term bonds and interest rates rise, you could stand to lose quite a bit of principal. That's because the longer the maturity of a bond or bond fund, the more the principal changes (both downward and upward) in reaction to a change in interest rates. On the other hand, if you had laddered your maturities by owning some short- and/or intermediate-term bond funds as well, you wouldn't have been hit as badly as a result of a rise in interest rates.

Specialized Funds

Specialized funds offer mutual fund investors even more choice. But be careful—the more specialized a fund becomes, the riskier it can be.

Balanced Funds These maintain a "balanced" combination of common stocks, bonds, and perhaps preferred stocks. They provide diversification between stocks and bonds in the same fund with a low minimum investment and are thus a good investment for someone with a small amount to invest.

One of the advantages of balanced funds and a major reason they have done so well as long-term investments is the forced discipline that they impose on the fund manager. As stock prices rise, the fund manager is forced to sell stocks to bring the portfolio back into balance. Conversely, if stock prices decline, the fund manager will be purchasing stock to bring the fund back into balance. Thus, the manager is forced to "buy low" and "sell high." Would that all of us could enforce that discipline upon our investments! Actually, I hope you will. I'll show you how to rebalance in Chapter 4. Balanced funds are the one fund to own if you own only one fund. (They're a great IRA investment, too.)

Sector Funds These invest only in the stocks of a single industry, such as biotechnology, waste management, utilities, or energy. Sector funds, unlike the typical mutual fund, zero in on a particular industry that may or may not have attractive prospects. The lack of diversity across industries means that sector funds can rapidly change from excellent to abysmal performance. Sector funds behave more like individual stocks than diversified funds, and selection of a sector fund cannot be made by using the same criteria (such as past track record) that usually guide the purchase of funds.

Don't be surprised if you see sector funds dominating the list of high-performing mutual funds over the past quarter or year. But before rushing to make an investment, realize that you'll probably find this fund ranked among the worst performers a year later. That's the way sector funds work.

But if you absolutely, positively have to play the sector fund game, see my tips for doing so on pages 43–44.

It's a Matter of Style

Within each of the stock fund categories—growth, growth and income, small company, and international—fund managers adopt one of three "management styles":

Growth Managers who favor growth investing choose companies whose revenues and earnings are accelerating. These companies are often the best performers in bull markets.

Value Managers of value funds favor companies whose stocks are undervalued. Perhaps the companies are temporarily out of favor with Wall Street or they possess unusually valuable, but as yet unrecognized assets. Value stocks usually don't perform as well as growth stocks in rapidly rising markets, but they also don't fall as much in declining markets.

Blend Finally, some managers prefer to find investment opportunities wherever they lurk, so they will use a blend of both growth investing and value investing.

When evaluating funds for possible additions to your portfolio, be sure to find out the fund manager's investment style. The easiest way to find out is to check one of the mutual fund monitoring services at the library. Aggressive investors tend to favor funds that utilize the growth style, more conservative investors prefer value funds, and, finally, some prefer managers who mix it up. Finally, investors who want to hedge their bets may select one growth-style fund and one value-style fund in each stock fund category.

CHAPTER 3

———∞∞∞———

STEP THREE: Selecting and Monitoring Your Mutual Fund Investments

Now that you have decided how you want to allocate your mutual fund investments between stocks and bonds, and you have decided how to divvy up your money among the various categories of stock and bond mutual funds, it's time to select good mutual funds in each category and then monitor your fund investments periodically. These tasks are covered in this chapter.

Selecting Good Funds

The process of selecting good funds may seem overwhelming. After all, there are thousands available, and the financial press is constantly highlighting hot-performing funds. In fact, every fund manages to find some performance measure that it can beat, so it may seem that, depending on how you measure them, all funds are good funds. But they're not. Yet there are hundreds of excellent funds, and the challenge is finding the ones that are right for you.

Selecting good funds is really not very difficult. If you have access to the right resources, and your library almost certainly does, you can find the right funds for you in a very short time. If you rely on someone else to recommend a fund, be sure to ask why he or she is high on the fund, especially if you are paying for the advice. In my experience, I have rarely encountered a situation where a paid adviser is recommending sub par funds. In fact, when asked to review a portfolio of mutual funds prepared by a broker or other adviser, I almost always have nothing but praise for the selections.

An Abundance of Resources

If you want to select your own funds, the best thing to do is to go to the library and check out one of the mutual fund monitoring services such as *Morningstar* or the *Value Line Mutual Fund Survey*. Also, the major financial newspapers, particularly *The Wall Street Journal* and *Barron's*, and the financial magazines, including *Business Week, Forbes, Fortune, Kiplinger's Personal Finance, Money, Smart Money,* and *Worth* provide regular coverage of mutual funds and periodic coverage that highlights the best. I particularly like the Friday edition of *The Wall Street Journal*, which provides detailed coverage and ranking on mutual fund performance, and the quarterly mutual fund wrap-ups published in both *The Wall Street Journal* and *Barron's* shortly after the end of each quarter.

While the above-mentioned magazines provide extensive fund coverage, be very careful about blindly following their recommended mutual funds. History has shown time and again that some of the funds they tout end up being short-term wonders whose fortunes change right after you or I buy the fund. On the other hand, lists of recommended funds can provide a good source of names for your further investigation.

The important thing is not to purchase a fund blindly just because you read about it in a magazine or newspaper or heard someone tout it. The same goes for mutual fund newsletters. While they can be an excellent source of ideas about good funds to invest in, you still need to do your homework.

How to Find Winning Funds

Let me go through the process that I've been using for years to find good mutual funds. If you do this, your main problem will be deciding which of several good funds that you find in each mutual fund category to buy.

First Identify Strong Candidates

There are several ways to identify possible fund candidates worthy of including in your portfolio. As mentioned earlier, the financial press bombards us with lists of top performers. Friends or co-workers might offer names. Or, you may want to do some of the legwork yourself by referring to one of the mutual fund monitoring services at the library. Also, you could refer to the Friday edition of *The Wall Street Journal,* which provides performance data and rankings. The following is an example of how each fund is identified and ranked in the Friday *Wall Street Journal.* For an explanation of the abbreviations, see the sidebar on pages 104–108.

If you're starting from scratch in locating good funds, check either the mutual fund monitoring services or *The Wall Street Journal.* Use the following criteria as a first cut.

Morningstar   Funds with an overall ranking of four or five stars. If a particular fund category has very few funds ranked four or five stars, consider selecting three-star funds.

The Value Line Mutual Fund Survey   Funds with an overall ranking of one or two. If a particular fund category has very

NAV	Net Chg	Fund Name	Inv Obj	YTD %ret	4Wk %ret	Total Return 1Yr-R	3Yr-R	5Yr-R	Max Init Chrg	Exp Ratio
XYZ MUTUAL FUND CO.										
10.01	...	Advfg	SB	+2.9	+0.6	+6.5 A	+5.8 A	+7.2 A	0.00	0.80
12.76	+0.02	AmUtil	SE	+3.2	+2.9	+24.0 B	NA ..	NS ..	0.00	0.50
10.47	−0.02	AsiaPc	IL	+10.6	+0.6	+17.5 B	NS ..	NS ..	0.00	2.00
19.97	−0.03	AsfAlc	MP	+3.1	−0.9	+13.6 D	+9.7 D	+10.7 D	0.00	1.20
20.64	−0.01	CmStk	GR	+8.6	−2.8	+22.7 C	+17.0 B	+21.5 A	0.00	1.20
10.32	+0.01	CorpBd	AB	−1.8	+1.2	+7.0 A	+8.8 A	+10.9 A	0.00	1.10
17.12	−0.05	Discov	CP	−1.9	−7.5	+13.1 E	+13.6 D	+15.9 C	0.00	1.40
11.30	...	EqInc	EI	+13.7	−1.0	NS ..	NS ..	NS ..	0.00	NA
10.23	+0.01	GovSc	LG	−2.7	+0.6	+3.8 B	+5.3 A	+9.3 A	0.00	0.90
18.54	−0.17	Growth	GR	+16.8	−6.7	+37.8 A	NS ..	NS ..	0.00	1.40
10.92	...	HYBond	HC	+14.0	+1.5	NS ..	NS ..	NS ..	0.00	NA
9.37	−0.01	HiYiMu	HM	−2.1	+0.7	+4.0 E	NS ..	NS ..	0.00	0.40
10.05	...	InsMu	NM	−3.7	−0.1	+2.3 E	+1.9 E	NS ..	0.00	1.00
15.01	−0.02	Intl	IL	+14.9	+2.2	+24.3 A	+16.8 A	NS ..	0.00	1.80
11.32	...	IntlBd	WB	+0.4	+0.5	+0.5 E	NS ..	NS ..	0.00	0.00
5.00	+0.01	MunAdv	SM	+2.1	+0.6	NS ..	NS ..	NS ..	0.00	NA
9.01	−0.01	MunBd	GM	−2.8	+0.3	+2.8 E	+2.6 E	+7.2 C	0.00	0.80
35.38	−0.06	Oppty	GR	+7.6	−2.3	+19.8 D	+15.8 C	+18.3 A	0.00	1.30
46.97	−0.09	SchaferV	GI	+9.4	−0.8	+21.4 D	+16.8 B	+19.7 A	0.00	1.28
12.55	...	SmCap	SC	+25.6	−4.8	NS ..	NS ..	NS ..	0.00	NA
9.67	...	ST Bd	SB	+1.7	+0.4	+6.5 A	+5.0 A	+7.3 A	0.00	0.90
10.51	...	STGlbl	WB	+4.3	+0.5	+9.6 B	NS ..	NS ..	0.00	0.00
9.64	−0.01	STMun	SM	+1.2	+0.4	+5.0 A	+2.6 E	NS ..	0.00	0.80
29.78	−0.13	Total	GI	+5.4	−4.7	+17.2 E	+13.6 D	+14.9 C	0.00	1.20
11.04	−0.02	Value	GR	+10.9	−1.9	NS ..	NS ..	NS ..	0.00	NA

few funds ranked one or two, consider selecting funds with an overall rank of three.

The Wall Street Journal Funds whose performance over the past one, three, and five years has earned a rank of A, B, or C. But don't select a fund if it has earned a C in more than one of those three time periods.

If you identify a potential fund from a magazine or from an acquaintance's recommendation, check the fund in both the Friday *Wall Street Journal* and *Morningstar* or *Value Line.* If you find a potential fund in the Friday *Wall Street Journal,* also check its *Morningstar* or *Value Line* ranking.

If you find a potential fund in either *Morningstar* or *Value Line,* also check its performance in the Friday *Wall Street Journal.* The key to finding good funds is to find funds that are considered superior in their particular categories using more than one source of mutual fund evaluation and performance.

Icing on the Cake

The more ranking services you can use to check on a particular fund, the better. Perhaps you could look at what both *Morningstar* and *Value Line* think of the fund. Or you could go to some of the financial magazines that periodically provide mutual fund ratings such as *Forbes* and *Business Week*. Ideally, you should be able to identify a fund that not only consistently ranks above average in comparison with its peers but that is also highly considered by the various ratings services you find in the library. Each of these services uses different criteria to evaluate past fund performance. So if you find a fund in a particular category that is well regarded by all of them, you have indeed found a wonderful fund.

If you would rather have me do the work for you, I'd be happy to send you my latest All-Star List of wonderful mutual funds. See page 225.

Additional Tips on Identifying and Purchasing Good Funds

Here are some suggestions to help you avoid mistakes when making mutual fund selections.

Should Big Funds Be Avoided Altogether?   There are a lot of observers of the mutual fund scene who contend that big funds—those with over $500 million or $1 billion in assets—should be avoided altogether. After all, they argue, when a fund gets to be that size, it's very difficult to be nimble. The analogy of trying to maneuver a supertanker is popular among the "don't own big funds" devotees.

But the facts don't support the notion that big funds underperform smaller funds, at least when considering mutual funds that invest in large-company (as opposed to small-company) stocks. I've studied the record many times over the years and have found that among large-company stock funds, bigger funds actually do better than smaller funds. So, when it comes to large growth funds and growth and income funds, bigger would seem to be better. On the other hand, the argument against investing in big funds has more validity for small-company funds because a large fund that concentrates in small-cap stocks may take very large positions in individual stocks. Large holdings of volatile small-company stocks may be difficult to sell quickly. That's why so many small-company stock funds close their doors to new investors when their managers feel that the fund is becoming too large.

Should You Invest in New Funds?   Personally, I won't invest in a fund that hasn't been around for at least five years. I like to see how these funds have performed—relative to their peers—in both good and bad markets. Nevertheless, some investors are attracted to new funds, particularly where they have been started by managers who have already achieved a stellar track record with other funds or other fund companies. Some studies have indicated that new funds tend to outperform established funds for a short period of time— the first year or so after the fund opened. Unfortunately, during subsequent years the same funds have a more difficult time sustaining their good performance. So the best advice for venturesome investors is that it may be worth buying a new fund run by an established fund manager, but you should monitor its performance more regularly than you might with a fund that has been around for many years.

Avoid the Capital Gains Trap When Buying a Fund
Like pumpkins that ripen in autumn, the capital gains in stock mutual funds are nearly ready to be picked toward the end of the year. But buying a fund just before it declares a capital

gain distribution could saddle you with tax obligations earned on investments before you even bought the fund. Here's how that works: Throughout the year most stock funds will buy and sell stocks and realize capital gains on these stocks. At the end of the year, unless the fund has an offsetting tax-loss carry forward from a previous year, these capital gains are declared and distributed to investors either in cash or additional shares if you reinvest. At the same time, fund shares are repriced—down, by the amount of the distribution. Therefore, the total value of an investment in the fund, if the capital gain distribution is reinvested, won't have changed as a result of the declaration. Getting into a fund at the wrong time can give instant revenue to the government.

EXAMPLE: Oscar Eagerman plunged into Lots-of-Profit Growth Fund on Christmas Eve with a purchase of 500 shares at $20 per share. Then on December 26, Lots-of-Profit declares a 20 percent capital gain distribution and, since Eagerman elected to have his capital gains reinvested, he receives the capital gain in additional shares. The share price is adjusted downward 20 percent—or $4 per share—from $20 to $16 since the fund has distributed 20 percent of its assets as a result of the capital gain.

Eagerman's $10,000 investment would still be worth $10,000. His $2,000 capital gain distribution was reinvested into 125 new shares ($2,000 ÷ $16 per share = 125 shares). This gives him a total of 625 shares worth $16 per share (625 × $16 = $10,000). But he would still owe capital gains taxes on the $2,000 the fund gave back to him in new shares. In essence Eagerman paid taxes on his pro rata share of the fund's entire year's capital gains even though he owned the shares for only a few days.

A good rule is not to jump into a fund during the final two months of the year if (1) it's been a good year for the fund and (2) this fund typically declares large capital gains during good years. The mutual fund monitoring services will show past capital gains distributions as well as the date when the fund declared these distributions. Alternatively, the fund company itself should provide this information if you call.

To Reinvest or Not to Reinvest, That Is the Question When you buy a fund you'll be asked whether or not you want to reinvest capital gains in dividend distributions. In general, this makes sense because you simply want your investments to continue growing, and one of the best ways is by reinvesting regularly. So you'll certainly want to reinvest in your retirement accounts (record keeping is easy here because all of the reinvested dividends and capital gains will be taxable when you withdraw money from a retirement account). And, if you have the discipline to keep good records, you should probably reinvest in your taxable investment accounts as well. But you will have to maintain meticulous records because when you sell all or part of a fund, you'll have to figure the cost basis of the shares you sold, including the cost basis of all the reinvested dividends and capital gains. This can be a computational nightmare, so be forewarned. If you are a lousy record keeper or don't want to put up with the hassle, then you are probably better off not reinvesting in a taxable investment account.

Monitoring Fund Performance

One of the beauties of mutual funds is that you are paying someone else a small amount of money (about $30 per year for a $5,000 investment) to lie awake at night worrying about how your money should be invested. But you still need to check up periodically on how the funds you own are doing. As you'll see, it's very simple, and it is important. You don't want to discover five years from now that the wonderful fund you bought has turned into a stinker.

How Often?

It's usually sufficient to review how your funds have performed every six months. If you really want to get into your investments, you might do it quarterly, but those who review their investments too regularly are likely to overreact to what they see as a disappointing problem. The fact is, every fund, even the best ones, will periodically underperform its peers. If you are checking a fund every month and you see that it is underperforming every month, you're liable to pull the trigger on the fund just before it—as so often happens with good funds—comes roaring back and produces quarter after quarter of stellar returns. So review your funds about every six months and certainly no less frequently than once each year.

How to Review Your Funds

Reviewing fund performance only takes a few minutes, and it is critical to ensuring that your investment program remains on track. You need to make sure the performance of each fund you own is up to snuff. That doesn't necessarily mean that a fund you own must have outperformed its peers over the past six months, but it is important to know if it has badly underperformed its peers. And it is also important to make sure that your stock and bond allocations remain on target.

Here, then, are the five steps for making a periodic evaluation of your fund holdings.

1. List all of your fund investments. Organize the list according to investment category—growth, small company, U.S. government bond, etc.

2. Determine what the total return performance of each fund has been during the most recent period. Note this performance next to the fund names on your summary. The financial newspapers will list the total return performance of each fund for the year-to-date (YTD).

3. Compare each fund's performance to the performance of its peer group. This peer group performance record can be found in the summaries that the mutual fund monitoring services provide or in *The Wall Street Journal* or *Barron's*. Make sure that you are accurately comparing each fund with its peer group average. The best source of peer group performance data is either the Friday *Wall Street Journal* or the average mutual fund performance data that appears each week in *Barron's*. The mutual fund monitoring services do not break down mutual fund categories to the extent that *The Wall Street Journal* and *Barron's* do. Comparing a fund's performance against its peers can be particularly problematic with bond funds. Many organizations that compile performance data lump all maturities of bond funds—short-term, intermediate-term, and long-term—into a single group. This means that, depending on how interest rates have changed over the period you are measuring, an otherwise good short-term or intermediate-term bond fund might be unfairly penalized compared with long-term bond funds that flourished over the period and whose superior performance is lumped in with all bond funds. Or the opposite could happen. Be particularly careful to assure that your bond funds—and all funds for that matter—are evaluated against the average of *similar* funds.

4. Gather more historical performance data for laggards. If you are concerned that your fund has underperformed its peer group average, review its performance over the past two years. The easiest way to obtain this information is to refer to the mutual fund monitoring services that rank each fund, by quintile, compared to its peers. If you determine your fund has been a laggard for a lot more than just the last six months, this may be the time to consider a change. On the other hand, if it has just now begun to lag, you should probably wait a while to see if, as is often the case, the fund rebounds.

5. Finally, determine your investment allocation status. It is important to summarize your investment allocation status as part of your periodic review. It's as simple as comparing the percentage of total fund assets in each investment category with your investment allocation objectives. If you find a significant variance between where your investments stand and your target, you should consider rebalancing to return to your target percentages. See Chapter 4 for information on how to rebalance.

Adios: Deciding to Sell a Fund

What's the best advice when deciding to sell a fund? Don't be too quick. Consider the following unfortunate but surprisingly common scenario. An investor chooses a stock mutual fund based solely on its strong past performance. Over the next few quarters, however, the fund's performance begins to lag compared to its peers. Disappointed, the investor sells in favor of another fund with a strong past performance. Shortly thereafter, the fund that was sold begins to rebound and once again posts the solid results for which the investor originally purchased it, while the recently purchased fund begins to lag. To such an investor it must seem as if he can do no right. In this case the problem was not with the funds but with the investor. And the problem is knowing when to sell.

When Does It Make Sense to Sell?

There are several factors that would make selling a fund appropriate. If a fund's performance deteriorates, as in the case described above, it is of critical importance to assess the cause of the poor performance. Investors who buy a fund on the basis of its investment style must judge the fund according to how well it is executing that style. See page 26 for a discussion of investment style. Just as trading a short stop for failing to hit enough home runs makes little sense to a major league baseball manager, selling a value fund for failing to keep pace with a roaring bull market that is particularly well-suited to growth-style funds makes little sense to an informed mutual fund investor.

Worse is the investor who sells a fund that is doing well in its category, but its category happens to be going through a tough time. If stock funds have made 10 percent so far this year and bond funds have lost 4 percent, you may think that a bond fund that has lost 2 percent doesn't belong in your portfolio. But, as you learned earlier, allocating your investments appropriately—and this includes bond funds as well as stock funds—is far more important to your investment success than trying to chase what seems to be the hottest fund category.

In particular, a fund that seems to be consistently underperforming its peers clearly becomes a sell candidate. Here's the rule I've used successfully for many years:

Never sell a fund on the basis of underperformance unless and until it has underperformed its peer group average for two consecutive years.

If you spend some time selecting really good funds, chances are that you will rarely have to sell a fund on the basis of this rule.

You may have to sell a fund simply to raise cash or to rebalance your portfolio. In these instances, there are obviously some funds that you may like more than others. Compare their performance and, if you have to sell a portion of a fund, sell the fund that is least attractive to you at the present time. Of course when you sell a fund you need to be mindful of your overall investment allocation and, if you are selling a fund out of a taxable, as opposed to a retirement, account you need to pay some attention to what taxes might be owed on the fund if and when you sell it.

But whatever your reason, the decision about whether or not to sell is far simpler if you understand why you purchased the fund in the first place. From that point on, you need only monitor the fund to make sure that the reasons for which it was purchased are still in force. The tendency of some investors to overtrade brings to mind a study conducted in the late 1980s that correlated the practice of stock fund managers to the performance of their funds. The one trait that was unmistakably correlated to success was discipline. It is a trait you would be wise to look for in your funds, and in yourself.

What Should You Do If Your Fund Changes Managers?

I daresay more ink has been wasted on the issue of what to do when a fund changes managers than on any other single investment subject. There are a lot of observers who say you should dump a fund if it changes managers. I'm not one of them. It's a little far-fetched to think that a fund company is going to replace the manager of a solid-performing fund (after all, those are the only kinds of funds you would own) with some slouch. Usually, the new manager proves to be up to the task. But that doesn't mean you should blithely ignore a change in fund manager. Instead, you would be well advised to monitor the fund's performance under the new captain a bit more frequently than you would for your stable of other funds. Moreover, if the fund produces a couple of quarters of subpar performance under the new manager, you may want to sell all or part of the fund a little more quickly than you would sell a fund under more normal circumstances.

Index Funds Can Play a Role in Your Portfolio

Index funds have arrived on the scene. Many investors, especially inexperienced investors and those with insufficient time to devote to following their investments, have found the indexing idea appealing. What is an index fund? Quite simply, it is a mutual fund that is designed to mimic a particular stock or bond index, the Standard & Poor's 500 Stock Index, for example. Proponents of indexing argue that it is futile for mutual funds to try to beat the market. Studies show that few experienced investment managers consistently beat the market indexes. So why pay a manager when simply buying a fund that equals the market average will work just as well—if not better?

Advantages of Indexing

Index funds offer a number of advantages, including low expenses. Because index funds are passively managed, there is no need to pay expensive analysts or managers for doing research, so the annual expenses for an index fund are much lower than those of actively managed funds. Index funds have also posted excellent performance. But remember, the market in general has been up since index funds have become particularly popular, and it is in up markets where they will do very well. Finally, index funds are broadly diversified across many industries. For investors with a limited amount of money to invest, index funds can be an excellent way to achieve diversification.

The Limitations of Indexing

With all the compelling advantages of indexing, however, indexing is not the magic solution to all of your investment needs. For example, you must be happy to achieve average market returns, because this is the best an index fund will do. Index fund managers are usually prohibited from using any defensive measures, such as moving out of stocks if the manager thinks stock prices are going to decline. So index funds will not be able to protect your investment in the event of a market downturn. Thus, in comparison with some actively managed stock funds that periodically take defensive measures when the market turns down, index funds tend to be more volatile.

Types of Index Funds

Index funds are now available in a host of flavors, designed to appeal to just about any particular interest of investors. Here are some of the more popular flavors:
- S&P 500 index funds
- Wilshire 5000 stock index funds
- Small-company index funds
- International stock index funds
- Bond index funds

Making Sense (and Dollars) Out of So Many Choices

Do the many permutations and combinations of index funds offer the same advantages of the granddaddy—the S&P 500 Index Funds? Unfortunately, conclusive answers have not yet been found. Some reports have indicated that actively managed small-company funds and actively managed international stock funds have a better chance of outperforming their respective indexes. Analysts believe that there is more opportunity for managers to identify attractive investments in the small company and international stock markets than there is in the U.S. large-company stock markets. So, while indexing has evolved into a very respectable method of investing, the results are mixed. For some markets, indexing has worked very well, but not as well in others. In all, index funds could certainly play a role in your investment accounts. You may first want to anchor a portion of your portfolio in an S&P 500 index fund. But remember that appropriate investment allocation calls for more than indexing, and indexing is more than buying just one index fund.

Assembling a Well-Balanced Portfolio That Includes Index Funds

Precisely by what percentage, if any, to index a portfolio varies with each investor. You may have time constraints. The less time you have to devote to selecting and monitoring your investments, the more sense index funds make. Although there isn't a clear-cut recommendation for everybody, the following table shows a sample portfolio that utilizes index funds. The proportion of index funds to actively managed funds varies in accordance with the past track records of index funds in the various categories. While index funds have proven to be very effective—large-cap U.S. stocks in particular—more of the portfolio is weighted toward indexing. (Here is where an S&P 500 index fund would fill the bill.) Where actively managed funds still offer advantages over indexing—small-caps and foreign stocks—actively managed funds are emphasized. But in all investment categories in the following table, index funds are used as an anchor for each category.

Should investors who have neither the time nor the experience to manage their own portfolios put all their money into index funds and forget about them? While this is definitely preferable to simply letting the money languish in low-return investments such as money market funds, it is also preferable to buying a group of mutual funds and then never monitoring their performance. But investors who index all of their investments will probably have to be satisfied with a somewhat lower return than they could have gained by selecting and monitoring both actively managed and index funds.

Table 3–1

Sample Portfolio That Incorporates Index Funds

	Index funds %	Actively managed funds %	Total %
STOCK FUNDS			
Growth	5	5	10
Growth and income	15	10	25
Small company	5	10	15
International	5	10	15
Subtotal stock funds	30	35	65
BOND FUNDS			
U.S. government/municipal/corporate	20	15	35
Total	50	50	100

Note: This sample portfolio is for an investor who wants an investment allocation of 65 percent stocks and 35 percent bonds.

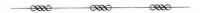

A Simple Strategy for Investing Profitably in Sector Funds

A sector fund (also known as a specialized fund) is not a mutual fund in the pure sense. While the fund is diversified insofar as it invests in stocks of many companies, a sector fund restricts those investments to a single industry such as financial services or computer companies or chemical companies. So while a garden variety mutual fund that is diversified across several different industries won't suffer too much if a particular industry falls on hard times, a sector fund that's in that hapless industry could suffer big time.

So I usually discourage investors from putting much, if any, money into a sector fund. Sometimes I feel I am fighting a losing battle, because sector funds almost always dominate the lists of best-performing mutual funds over a past quarter or past year. That shouldn't come as a surprise, because if a particular sector is flying high, chances are that the sector fund will be beating the daylights out of the more diversified funds. All too often, however, that same high-performing sector fund ends up on next year's list of worst-performing funds. That's the way it is with an undiversified investment.

If, in spite of my admonitions, you become tempted to put some money in sector funds, please don't bet the ranch on them. Put no more than 5 to 10 percent of your portfolio into sector funds. Also, please don't buy a sector fund because it was a recent high performer. I'll guarantee you'll be financially worse off if you do so. Instead, pick a sector fund because you are excited by the prospects for stocks of a particular sector, in other words, a particular industry. And this leads me to my strategy.

Strategy

My strategy for investing in sector funds involves first identifying industries that are considered to have very attractive prospects over the next year or so. There are a couple of ways to do this. If you have an account with a full-service brokerage firm, your broker may be able to provide you with some reports that identify attractive industries. Or, you could go to the library and check out the *Value Line Investment Survey,* which ranks over ninety different industries for probable performance over the next year. But whatever your source, if the industry is expected to do well, you could then go about the task of identifying a good sector fund in that industry. This process is no different from the process of locating any good mutual fund. Be forewarned, however, that in spite of the popularity of sector funds, funds are not yet available for many industry categories. Here, however, are some industries that have a sufficient number of sector funds available so as to enable you to identify a good one:

- Energy/natural resources
- Financial services
- Health care
- Precious metals
- Real estate
- Technology
- Utilities

Three for the Money

In spite of my overall reservations about sector funds, I have to admit an attraction to three particular sectors. In fact, I think most investors, once they've got enough money to invest in each of the general mutual fund categories that I recommend, should strongly consider investing in these three important and attractive industrial sectors:

1. Health-care funds. You might think that with all of the problems the health-care industry is going through that this is an industry to be avoided. But there are a lot of health-care companies that are in the business not only of improving our health but also of reducing the costs of keeping us healthy and treating illness. It takes a pro to separate the good health-care stocks from the also-rans. That's what you'll get when you buy a solid health-care fund.

2. Real estate funds. There are three major long-term investment categories: stocks, bonds, and real estate. While most investors can't afford to buy real estate, real estate mutual funds are an easy and inexpensive way to add this important investment category to your portfolio. See Chapter 14 for more information on real estate investing.

3. Technology funds. I really like the prospects for the technology industry over the next decade. In fact, I think we're in the midst of a major transition away from the old industrial companies that are so heavily represented among blue chip stocks. A whole new generation of wonderful companies will take their place. What industry will these companies be in? Without a doubt, technology. But it's very difficult to put together a well-diversified portfolio of individual stocks in the volatile and rapidly changing technology industry. So the best way to play this exciting sector is with a technology mutual fund, and there are many good ones out there.

CHAPTER 4

STEP FOUR: Periodically Rebalancing Your Investment Allocation

If you follow my first three steps you will achieve very good investment results. Step four, periodically rebalancing your investment allocation, will transform you from achieving very good investment results to achieving excellent investment results. The reason for this is quite simple. Rebalancing your investments forces you to do the right thing. Often it requires you to go against the current outlook of Wall Street experts. Going against the Wall Street crowd is often not a bad thing to do, and rebalancing allows you to do just that. Here's how rebalancing works.

About every six months, total your investments and check to see how they're allocated. In other words, figure out what the current percentages are in each of your investment categories. Chances are that you'll find that the percents you now have in stocks and bonds varies from the allocation you want. That's because stock and bond values fluctuate, of course. What rebalancing does is bring your investment allocation back to the percentages you determined in Steps one and two in Chapters 1 and 2. Let's look at a brief example:

EXAMPLE: Say you want a 60 percent stock/40 percent bond overall allocation. But stock prices have risen over the past six months to the point where stocks now account for 67 percent of your portfolio's total value. What should you do? Rebalance by selling enough of your stock investments and use that money to add more to your bond investments so that you bring your portfolio back to your 60 percent stock/ 40 percent bond target allocation. By periodically rebalancing your portfolio, you force yourself to invest very sensibly. In this example, the stock market has risen rather sharply over the past six months and you're selling some of your stocks after they've risen in value. This would not be a bad time to be selling *a small amount* of your stock investments. Of course, if the market has risen sharply, the investment experts are flooding the airwaves with a very rosy outlook. You're probably selling some of your stocks at a time when the great majority of investors are buying stocks. But that's okay. Rebalancing also forces you to add to stocks if the stock market has fallen and add to bonds when interest rates have risen. These are all very sensible things to do.

How Often Should You Rebalance?

You might be thinking that if rebalancing is such a great thing, you should be rebalancing frequently. Certainly you should rebalance soon if there have been major changes in the market (more on that later), but, since rebalancing takes some time, you don't want to burden yourself with it. While rebalancing once a year may be appropriate for many investors, my recommendation is to rebalance about every six months *unless* there has been a major change in either stock prices or interest rates (which affect bond prices) since the last time you rebalanced. Here's my rule: If, since the last time you rebalanced, stock prices have moved up or down by more than 10 percent (use any of the major stock indexes such as the Dow Jones Industrial Average or the S&P 500 as your benchmark), then I would rebalance immediately. Also, if interest rates have moved rapidly up or down by greater than 1 percent since your last rebalancing, I would again rebalance the portfolio immediately. The easiest interest rate measure to use is the yield on the thirty-year U.S. Treasury bond, which is the bellwether bond interest rate indicator and is regularly published in the financial pages of the newspaper.

How Do You Go About Rebalancing?

You may have read about the importance of rebalancing your investments, but chances are you haven't received any guidance on how to do it. This has led a lot of investors to lament, "Rebalancing is great in theory, but how is it done in practice?" Well, I'll show you how it's done. Almost anyone with rudimentary math and calculator skills can figure out how to rebalance his or her portfolio.

Step 1:   Write down the target investment allocation you set for your portfolio the last time you rebalanced. (If this is the first time you're rebalancing, write down the target investment allocations you have established for yourself in Chapters 1 and 2.) Table 4–1 provides an example of a portfolio allocation of six months ago. (We'll assume in these illustrations that we last rebalanced in January, and it's now July.)

Next, consider whether you should change these target allocation percentages. While you should avoid making any major changes in your target allocation percentages, you may want to make small changes in the allocation periodically, usually to account for your advancing years. (Don't get depressed,

---------- **Table 4–1** ----------

Rebalancing Your Portfolio

STEP 1

	Investment balances last January	Step1: Target allocation (%)
STOCK FUNDS		
Growth	$5,000	10
Growth and income	15,000	30
Small company	7,500	15
International	7,500	15
Subtotal stock funds	35,000	70
BOND FUNDS		
Government	$5,000	10
Municipal	5,000	10
Corporate	5,000	10
Subtotal bond funds	15,000	30
Total	$50,000	100

we're all advancing in years, and your children, nieces, and nephews are aging at a faster percentage rate than you are.)

Step 2: Summarize, by investment category, your current portfolio amounts and percentages. If, as may be the case, you have several different investment accounts, be sure to combine them for purposes of rebalancing your investments. Rebalancing doesn't accomplish much if you're rebalancing only part of your total investment holdings. See Columns A and B of Table 4–2 for a summary of current investment status.

Step 3: Calculate how much money you will need to add or subtract from each investment holding in order to rebalance the portfolio to your target allocation. Column C of Table 4–2 shows the target allocation percentages and Column D shows the amounts that need to be added to or subtracted from each investment category.

Here's how to come up with the amounts necessary to rebalance: Consider growth funds. The target allocation is 10 percent while the current allocation is 14 percent. Here's the math needed to determine how much the growth fund holdings need to be reduced to get them from 14 percent of the portfolio to 10 percent:

Current growth fund holdings	$7,455
Target growth fund holdings (10% × $54,990)	5,500
Reduction in growth fund holdings necessary to rebalance	$1,955

Here's the math for international funds:

Current international fund holdings	$7,265
Target international fund holdings (15% × $54,990)	8,250
Increase in international fund holdings necessary to rebalance	$ 985

Step 4: Rebalance the portfolio by adding or reducing enough of each fund to bring that fund back into balance with the target percentage. The result is a rebalanced portfolio, as shown in Column E of Table 4–2.

Some Important Things to Consider

While the mechanics of rebalancing are pretty straightforward, there are some other important matters to consider before you rebalance. Sometimes, the costs or inconvenience of rebalancing may outweigh the benefits.

Table 4–2

Rebalancing Your Portfolio

STEPS 2, 3, and 4

	STEP 2			STEP 3	STEP 4
	A. Current Balance (July)	**B.** Current Allocation (%)	**C.** Target Allocation (%)	**D.** Addition Reduction	**E.** Target Portfolio
STOCK FUNDS					
Growth	$7,455	14	10	($1,955)	$5,500
Growth and Income	16,695	30	30	(205)	16,490
Small company	9,670	18	15	(1,420)	8,250
International	7,265	13	15	985	8,250
Subtotal stock funds	$41,085	75	70	($2,595)	38,490
BOND FUNDS					
Government	$4,600	8	10	$ 900	5,500
Municipal	4,550	8	10	950	5,500
Corporate	4,755	9	10	745	5,500
Subtotal bond funds	13,905	25	30	2,595	16,500
Total	$54,990	100	100	$ 0	$54,990

Tax Consequences

Before rebalancing, carefully analyze what, if any, tax consequences would result. Avoid making sales where there may be costly tax consequences—selling a security that requires a large capital gain tax to be paid, for example. Instead, find alternatives that will result in your owing little or no taxes— rebalancing in a retirement account, perhaps, since no taxes are owed until you start withdrawing money from the retirement account.

Transaction Costs

Also be mindful of transaction costs. The benefits of rebalancing can soon be lost if fees and commissions eat away at your portfolio. Rebalancing through no-load funds or load fund families that allow no-cost switches within the family is the way to go.

Time

Finally, you may find that the necessary rebalancing involves such a small amount of money that it isn't worth your time and effort. Perhaps you should wait another six months before rebalancing. But you can't reach that conclusion without going through the process of finding out exactly where your portfolio stands. Finally, the process of rebalancing a large number of funds is a lot easier if you're rebalancing within a single fund family or through a brokerage account that combines mutual funds from several families such as those offered by Fidelity and Schwab.

PART II

∞∞∞

Adding Stocks and Bonds to Your Portfolio

CHAPTER 5

———∞∞∞———

Why You Should Be Investing in Individual Stocks and Bonds in Addition to Mutual Funds

Aren't Mutual Funds Enough?

Mutual funds offer a lot of advantages to investors. That's why I started you out with them. Their advantages include diversification of your investments at low cost, professional management, and generally lower investment fees, particularly for smaller portfolios. They're also a useful way to invest in specific categories that interest you and to invest in securities that otherwise might be very difficult to purchase and manage. International mutual funds, for example, are about the only feasible way for most investors to own stock in foreign companies. But mutual funds also have some disadvantages, in particular the lack of control over the timing of capital gains taxes and, with respect to bond mutual funds, the possibility that your fund could lose its value if interest rates rise.

Buying individual stocks and bonds allows you more control

over your investments. You have control over the timing of capital-gains tax recognition. As long as you hold on to a stock or bond, you owe no taxes on its appreciation in value. Also, buying individual bonds and holding on to them until they mature avoids the risk inherent in bond mutual funds that rising interest rates will cause of loss in value of the investment. True, your bonds will also lose value if interest rates rise, but that is of little importance if you hold on to your bonds until they mature.

But investments in stocks and bonds also have some disadvantages, including the time and expense necessary to manage them effectively. Municipal bonds, for example, can be particularly troublesome for individual investors because of the lack of current published price information. Also, it is very expensive to achieve adequate diversification in a portfolio of individual stocks and bonds.

But by combining both methods of investing—mutual funds and individual stocks and bonds—you can take advantage of the opportunities that both ownership methods offer. Once your investment portfolio reaches a level where you can afford individual investments, you should consider striking a balance between both methods to take advantage of the desirable features of each. Most successful long-term investors will invest in—and benefit from—both individual securities and mutual funds.

Before showing you how to fit individual stocks and bonds into your portfolio, let's first review the various categories of stocks and bonds. See Table 5–1.

Stock and Bond Glossary

Types of Common Stocks

Common stock investments offer two possible benefits. First, the company may pay dividends to its shareholders. Second,

--- Table 5–1 ---

The Best of Both Worlds— Combining Mutual Funds and Individual Securities

	STOCKS	BONDS
MUTUAL FUNDS	Stock mutual funds	Bond mutual funds
INDIVIDUAL SECURITIES	Individual stocks	Individual bonds

investors may benefit through capital appreciation—an increase of the share price of stock. Not all common stocks are the same, however. Some pay dividends, and some don't. Some have relatively stable prices, while others are more volatile. Most common stocks are classified into one of several categories.

Growth Stocks Investors buy growth stocks for capital appreciation. Because most growth companies are having to finance their growth and are involved in research, most or all of their earnings are reinvested in the company for future expansion. Therefore, while the shares of growth stocks have the prospect of increasing market value, they pay few, if any, dividends. The prices of growth stocks usually rise in value more than do those of other stocks, but they also decline in price more significantly.

Income Stocks Income stocks pay a higher-than-average dividend. Companies whose stocks fall into this category are typically in fairly stable industries (for example, telecommunications and utilities), have strong finances, and pay out a substantial portion of their earnings in dividends. Investors in income stocks also usually enjoy appreciation in the value of the stocks, and if the company's fortunes improve, the dividends will rise as well. While income stocks may not have the growth potential of growth stocks when prices are rising, they also tend not to decline in value as much as growth stocks when stock prices take a tumble.

Small-Company Stocks Small-company stocks are more speculative than the other stock categories discussed here. In a sense, all common stocks are speculative, since they offer a variable rather than fixed return like bonds. But small-company stocks are more speculative than large-company stocks because smaller companies are more susceptible to changing economic conditions, competition, and declining stock markets. While you may be in a position to afford taking a "flyer" on one or a few small company stocks, most investors should avoid committing too much money to individual small-company stocks. On the other hand, a small-company stock mutual fund is an important component of your investment portfolio.

International Stocks These are stocks of foreign companies. Many of the world's greatest companies are headquartered overseas. While buying shares of most foreign companies is very difficult for U.S. investors, many large overseas companies are listed on the U.S. stock exchanges and can be purchased in U.S. dollars. The shares of foreign companies that trade on U.S. stock exchanges are called ADRs, which stands for "American Depository Receipts." The easiest way to own international stocks is through an international stock mutual fund.

Types of Bonds

Bonds pay a fixed rate of interest, but their principal value can fluctuate depending upon whether interest rates in general are rising or falling. Visualize a seesaw. When interest rates rise, bond prices fall; when interest rates fall, bond prices rise. Here are the three major categories of bonds.

U.S. Government Bonds U.S. government bonds come in three varieties: Treasury bonds, mortgage-backed securities, and U.S. savings bonds.

TREASURY SECURITIES. These securities are the means by which the U.S. government borrows money. (As you know, Uncle Sam is pretty good at borrowing money.) Treasury bonds are issued by the U.S. government and are considered the safest of all bonds, since they are backed by the government. Treasury securities that are issued with a maturity of greater than five years are called Treasury bonds. Treasury securities that are issued with maturities of two to five years are called Treasury notes. Those of one year or less are called Treasury bills, and they're discussed in Chapter 17.

Uncle Sam has introduced a new species of Treasury bond, called "inflation-indexed bonds." While they pay a lower interest rate than regular Treasury bonds, the value of the bond is increased each year to account for inflation. Inflation-indexed Treasury bonds are certainly worth a look.

Treasury bills, notes, and bonds have a bit of a tax advantage. Interest earned on these bonds is not subject to state or local income taxes. There is one exception to this, which few investors realize. If you put a U.S. Treasury security or a U.S. Treasury mutual fund into a retirement account, interest that would otherwise not have been subject to state income taxes *will* become subject to state income taxes when you withdraw the money. The reason for this is that all income earned in a retirement account is subject to state income taxes. So you are better off keeping U.S. Treasury bonds outside of your retirement accounts in favor of corporate bonds, which are discussed below.

An interesting subspecies of U.S. Treasury securities, *zero-coupon bonds* (also called "stripped Treasury bonds") pay no interest along the way. Instead they are sold at a deep discount, which means they are sold at a price that is much lower than the maturity value of the bond. While you don't get any interest along the way, your profit comes at the end in the form of a big increase in the amount you are paid at maturity compared with your original investment.

The main advantage in zero-coupon bonds is that you are guaranteed a set rate of return insofar as the interest earned on these bonds is, in effect, reinvested at the original interest rate. Therefore, if interest rates decline you don't have to worry about reinvesting interest income at a lower rate. This automatic compounding also avoids your having to make decisions to invest the interest you would receive on a regular bond.

The main drawback of these "zeros" is that even though you are not receiving interest along the way, for tax purposes, the IRS assumes that you are, so you have to pay taxes on the "imputed" interest income. The upshot? These are good investments for tax-deferred retirement accounts such as IRAs and Keogh plans because you don't have to pay taxes on them before you retire. But is it worth putting zero-coupon Treasuries into a retirement account if you are going to subject the interest to state income taxes when you withdraw the money? I think it is, because the other advantages of zero-coupon Treasuries outweigh this drawback. But I still don't think you should put standard U.S. Treasury bonds or U.S. Treasury funds into a retirement account. Zeros are the exception.

MORTGAGE-BACKED SECURITIES. These securities have peculiar-sounding names like Ginnie Mae, Fannie Mae, and Freddie Mac. These investments represent pools of mortgages. Their relatively high interest rates have been attracting a lot of investor interest, but the high investment minimums—typically $25,000—mean that many of us can't afford them. If your pockets aren't that deep, you can get a piece of the mortgage-backed security action through a mortgaged-backed security mutual fund.

U.S. SAVINGS BONDS. U.S. savings bonds are a popular and inexpensive way for savers to invest in government securities. Unfortunately, the U.S. Treasury made savings bonds much less attractive back in 1995 when they changed the rules. While you should hold on to older savings bonds that are still paying attractive interest, I would avoid investing in them anymore. There are just too many better investment opportunities elsewhere. The only exception to this might be if you are using U.S. savings bonds to build a college fund, and if you are quite confident that when your child enters college, your income will fall under the limits so that you will be able to cash in the savings bonds and not pay income taxes on the accumulated interest. But that requires a pretty clear crystal ball.

Municipal Bonds   These bonds are issued by state and municipal governments to borrow money. With few exceptions, the interest earned on municipal bond investments is exempt from federal income taxes and in many instances from state and local taxes. Taxes take a heavy toll on your investments so it behooves you to take a close look at municipal bonds.

If you reside in a state that imposes high taxes on interest income, you should consider investing in municipals issued by your state. For example, if you reside in New York, interest on municipal securities issued by the state of New York or by New York municipalities would be exempt from both federal and state income taxes. These are known as "double tax-free" bonds. Interest on municipal securities issued by U.S. territories (the Territory of Guam and the Commonwealth of Puerto Rico) is generally exempt from both federal and state income taxes, no matter what state you reside in.

Because of the tax advantage, municipal bonds don't pay as high interest as U.S. government and corporate bonds. But that doesn't mean that munis are a raw deal. *Au contraire.*

It's not the stated interest that the bond pays that counts. It's how much you have left after taxes. (Of course, you would never put a municipal bond into a tax-advantaged retirement account because the bond interest itself is tax-exempt. If you put municipal bonds into a tax-deferred account, the interest that would otherwise have been tax-exempt would be subject to income taxes when you take the money out.)

Comparing the interest paid on municipal bonds with the interest paid on U.S. government or corporate bonds is quite simple. What you need to do is to calculate the "taxable equivalent yield" of a municipal bond. The formula for taxable equivalent yield enables you to compare a tax-free municipal bond investment to a taxable U.S. government or Treasury bond investment. Here's the formula:

$$\text{Taxable equivalent yield} = \frac{\text{municipal bond interest rate}}{(1 - \text{your federal income tax bracket})}$$

Let's look at an example.

EXAMPLE: Rhonda and Ron Ronsen are in the 28 percent federal income tax bracket. They're considering purchasing either a municipal bond paying 5 percent interest or a Treasury bond paying 6 percent interest. In order to compare the yields accurately, they must first compute the taxable equivalent yield on the municipal bond. Here's how they do it:

1. They need to convert their income tax bracket to its decimal equivalent: 28 percent becomes .28.
2. They need to apply the above formula to their situation.

$$\text{Taxable equivalent yield} = \frac{\text{municipal bond interest rate}}{(1 - \text{your federal income tax bracket})}$$

$$= \frac{5\%}{(1 - .28)} = \frac{5\%}{.72} = 6.9\%$$

For the Ronsens, the taxable equivalent yield of the munici-pal bond investment turns out to be 6.9 percent, compared with 6 percent for the Treasury bond. In other words, a Treasury bond would have to pay over 6.9 percent interest in order for the Ronsens to receive higher after-tax interest with a Treasury bond than they would with the 5 percent municipal bond. The tax-free investment has a lower interest rate but it provides more interest income than the taxable Treasury bond once taxes are factored in.

How safe are municipal bonds? Most municipal bonds are pretty safe. After all, states and municipalities have a lot of power to raise money. But some municipalities have defaulted, so it behooves you to buy only higher rated municipal bonds. Most municipal bonds are rated by one or more of the ratings agencies, such as Moody's and Standard & Poor's. Avoid any bonds that aren't rated.

Corporate Bonds   Corporations issue a variety of bonds, but, thanks to the ratings agencies, it's fairly easy to separate the junk bonds from the high-quality bonds. In fact, when you ask your broker to look for some corporate (or municipal) bonds, the first question she is likely to ask is, "What rating are you looking for?" Interest on corporate bonds is subject to both federal and state income taxes. Therefore, they usually pay somewhat higher interest than U.S. Treasury bonds (whose interest is exempt from state income taxes) and munic-ipal bonds (whose interest is exempt from federal and, per-haps, state income taxes). The high interest that corporate bonds pay makes them particularly attractive for retirement accounts, since you don't have to pay income taxes currently on the interest you receive from the bonds.

CHAPTER 6

——— ∞∞∞ ———

How to Fit Individual Stocks and Bonds into Your Investment Portfolio

Now that you understand the advantages of holding individual stocks and bonds in a portfolio, the next step is to examine how you might go about doing so. The extent to which you include individual stocks and bonds in your portfolio will largely depend on two matters: your personal preference and the amount of money you have to invest.

Your Personal Preference Investors differ about whether they prefer mutual funds over direct investments or vice versa, and that's fine, so long as you keep an open mind. I think that investors are best served by a combination of both investment methods, and I hope you won't reject individual bonds and particularly individual stocks because you think they're too complicated or too risky. They're not, as you'll see in Chapters 7 and 8. At the other extreme, I trust you won't reject mutual funds altogether, because mutual funds are the only way for most investors (unless you have a huge portfolio) to play important market segments, notably small-company and international stocks.

The amount of time you have available to monitor your investments will also influence your preferences for mutual funds and/or individual securities. In general, the less time you have to devote to your investments, the higher the proportion that should be invested in mutual funds, unless you want to use a broker or investment adviser to choose and manage individual stocks and bonds for you.

The Amount of Money You Have to Invest Unlike mutual funds, where you can begin investing with $3,000 or less, buying individual stocks and bonds requires considerably more money to achieve adequate diversification. You don't want to buy less than 100 shares of a particular issue (buying smaller quantities raises your transactions costs). Therefore, it would cost you $3,000 to buy 100 shares of a $30 stock (plus commissions). And that's just one stock. You really need at least four or five stocks in different industries to be adequately diversified. Bonds require an even higher price tag. Most experts suggest that you invest at least $10,000 in an individual corporate or municipal bond issue. Otherwise, you're likely to get a very poor price from the broker, since they really don't like to deal in such small denominations. Even $10,000 is considered small, so you really need to have a good rapport with your broker to be assured that when you buy a municipal or corporate bond you are getting a fair deal. While U.S. Treasury notes and bonds can be bought at lower denominations, you should probably steer clear of them unless you have at least $10,000.

Before you even consider buying individual securities, you should have assembled a portfolio of mutual funds in all of the categories that were discussed in Chapter 2. That will probably require somewhere between $25,000 and $40,000, so you should probably not consider investing in individual securities until you have at least that much money invested in mutual funds. After that point, you can certainly begin making forays into individual stocks. But with the high price tag for individual bonds, you should probably have at least $75,000 available to invest before plunging into individual bonds.

Sample Portfolios That Incorporate Both Mutual Funds and Individual Securities

Enough said about structuring an investment portfolio and selecting appropriate investments. Now, let's look at how this might be done in real life under three scenarios: a $50,000 portfolio, a $100,000 portfolio, and a $500,000 portfolio.

A $50,000 Portfolio

If you have $50,000 available to invest there is enough to begin investing in some individual stocks, although not yet enough to buy individual bonds. In the following table, which assumes an investment allocation of 70 percent stocks and 30 percent bonds, $15,000 is devoted to individual stocks. This should be enough to be able to own three or four different stocks in different industries. While this may not in itself, be enough to achieve the level of diversification you would like in the individual stocks, you also have $20,000 of stock mutual funds which are, of course, well diversified. So considering your stock total investments, you certainly should have sufficient diversification. See Table 6–1.

A $100,000 Portfolio

When a portfolio approaches six figures, investors who are interested in buying individual stocks and bonds should have enough money to be able to do so. In the following illustration, which assumes a 50 percent stock and 50 percent bond

--- **Table 6-1** ---

A $50,000 Portfolio

Investment allocation: 70% stocks and 30% bonds

	STOCKS	BONDS
MUTUAL FUNDS	Total stock funds: $20,000	Total bond funds: $15,000
INDIVIDUAL SECURITIES	Total individual stocks: $15,000	Total individual bonds: $0
	TOTAL STOCK AND STOCK FUNDS: $35,000	**TOTAL BONDS AND BOND FUNDS:** $15,000

investment allocation, I've split the total stock money in half so that it is equally divided between stock funds and individual stocks. On the bond side, I've skewed the weighting a bit toward individual bonds, since you will probably need around $10,000 to buy an individual bond issue. Here, then, an investor might be able to buy one U.S. Treasury bond, one municipal bond, and one corporate bond. Be cautious, however, if you adopt a similar approach toward buying individual bonds with a portfolio of this size. Be sure to limit your individual municipal and corporate bond purchases to highly rated issuers. (You don't need to worry about quality with Treasuries, since they are the safest of all bonds.) See Table 6–2.

Table 6-2

A $100,000 Portfolio

Investment allocation: 50% stocks and 50% bonds

	STOCKS	BONDS
MUTUAL FUNDS	Total stock funds: $25,000	Total bond funds: $20,000
INDIVIDUAL SECURITIES	Total individual stocks: $25,000	Total individual bonds: $30,000

TOTAL STOCK AND STOCK FUNDS:	$50,000	**TOTAL BONDS AND BOND FUNDS:**	$50,000

A $500,000 Portfolio

As the saying goes, the rich get richer. And one reason they get richer is that people with a lot of money to invest simply have more options. The following sample portfolio, which assumes a target investment allocation of 60 percent stocks and 40 percent bonds, has been split down the middle so that half of the stock and bond money is invested in funds and the other half is invested in individual stocks and bonds. Diversification within the individual stock and individual bond categories is quite easy when investments get to this level. Perhaps a dozen individual stocks could be owned and as many as ten individual bonds. If nothing else, this should be an incentive for you to save like crazy and invest those savings well so that you can eventually get your portfolio up to these lofty levels.

Tax considerations could also influence the way an investor with a large portfolio would array his or her investments. Often, investors with large portfolios find themselves in high tax brackets (you can't have everything). In these cases, buying and holding individual stocks and individual municipal bond issues will help reduce the tax bite.

With respect to bonds, special attention should be paid to buying bonds of different maturities. This strategy for buying bonds is further discussed on pages 79–80.

--- **Table 6-3** ---

A $500,000 Portfolio

Investment allocation: 60% stocks and 40% bonds

	STOCKS	BONDS
MUTUAL FUNDS	Total stock funds: $150,000	Total bond funds: $100,000
INDIVIDUAL SECURITIES	Total individual stocks: $150,000	Total individual bonds: $100,000
	TOTAL STOCKS AND STOCK FUNDS: **$300,000**	TOTAL BONDS AND BOND FUNDS: **$200,000**

CHAPTER 7

You Don't Need to Be a Pro to Pick Good Stocks and Bonds

You may be intimidated by the idea of going out and selecting a stock or a bond for your portfolio. A lot of people certainly are. And yes, it is more difficult—and often more risky—to buy a stock or a bond than it is to buy a mutual fund. But where there is risk there is opportunity. I think the opportunities outweigh the risks, particularly if you are willing to spend some time learning about stock and bond investing and keeping up-to-date with your investments. In my mind, that's one of the most profitable things you can do. Remember, it's your financial future.

Investing in Stocks

A lot of individuals think they have no place in today's stock market. With the big institutional investors, program trading, and "triple witching hours," it's no wonder that the small investor feels, well, "small." True, the market itself is no children's playground. You may be one of the millions of people who feel that the roller-coaster ride of stock investing is just too risky. Yes, it is a roller-coaster ride, but stocks have consistently proven to be the best inflation-beating investment around. These days if you don't beat inflation with your investments, you really don't stand a chance of making much headway in your financial life. So if you haven't invested in stocks, my advice to you is to learn about them, and then begin to invest in stocks *gradually*. There's no real rush, as long as you begin to add stocks to your investments. Incidentally, you may have nothing but disdain for stocks, but if you participate in a pension plan, you can bet that more than half of your pension plan's assets are invested in stocks.

Here are some tips on making good stock investments and avoiding costly mistakes.

• **Never buy stocks indiscriminately.** Far too many investors buy stocks haphazardly simply because they have money to invest or they feel they should buy a stock or they've received some hot tip from an acquaintance. This is a bad practice; stock investments should be made when you have a good reason to buy a particular stock.

• **Select a promising industry.** At any given time, most industries in the economy are either on the upswing or on the downswing. When choosing a stock to buy, you'll give that stock a good head start by selecting one that is in a promising industry. The *Value Line Investment Survey* ranks industries as well as stocks each week. In fact, it also ranks the best stocks within each of the most promising industries.

• **Diversify.** Try to own stocks in several different industries. The danger of having too many eggs in one basket can't be stressed too much. On the other hand, overdiversification with a small amount of money when you own individual stocks is unwise. You can keep track of five or ten stocks more easily than twenty-five stocks. Incidentally, studies have shown that investors can achieve excellent diversification with as few as ten to twelve stocks.

- **Buy good value.** There are two basic investment styles. *Growth* investors seek companies whose revenues and profits are growing rapidly. *Value* investors, on the other hand, search for companies that are undervalued by Wall Street. True, most of these companies are not sexy by Wall Street standards and some of them have recently gone through some hard times. But companies who stand a chance to make solid earnings growth in the future are every bit as attractive as the high-growth darlings of Wall Street. Value stocks also have another advantage—their downside risk potential is much lower than growth stocks. Investors in growth stocks certainly can make a lot of money in a short period of time, but they can also lose a lot of money quickly. I think growth stock investing is a full-time job. Owning a stable of value stocks, however, will allow you to sleep at night not having to worry about whether the next quarterly earnings report for your high-flying company is going to be below Wall Street predictions and, hence, the stock will lose a third of its value by noon.
- **Buy low and sell high.** Condition yourself to buy a stock when a company's share price is down and to sell it when the price is up. (See Chapter 8 for some guidance on when to sell a stock.) Suffice it to say that the best time to sell a stock is when it's hot (everybody wants to own it) and its price is high. This is the tried and true "buy low, sell high" rule.
- **Stay abreast of market trends.** It is always important when considering a stock to look at the general trend in the market and in that stock's industry. A stock that has already risen in value might be a good candidate for continued gains if the market is still rising. Conversely a stock that does not respond to a general market rise may turn out to be a poor investment.
- **Buy stocks in companies with strong dividend payment records.** Let me clue you in on how most of the rich people in this country got rich. They bought stocks in compa-

nies that had strong dividend payment records. These companies not only pay good dividends year in and year out, but they're also in the habit of raising the dividends along the way. So you get the best of both worlds with these stocks. First, the stock will appreciate in value over the years without your having to pay any capital gains taxes until you sell the stock—if you ever sell it. Second, you have a rising source of income to help you keep up with inflation over the decades. The rich get richer because they buy these stocks and probably die with them. The heirs then inherit the shares at whatever the value is as of the date of death. This is known as the "stepped-up" basis. In effect, no capital gains whatsoever are paid on the stock.

You should start doing the same. Buying stocks in companies that have a consistent history of paying generous dividends has another advantage. In a bear market, these companies have usually declined less in price than companies that paid no dividend at all or that paid dividends erratically, since investors are confident that the dividend will keep coming through thick and thin. To get an idea of how much these dividends can rise over the years, take a look at Table 7-1, which shows how much the dividends has increased in four widely held blue chip companies.

• **Use the "low P/E and high dividend" strategy.** Many successful long-term investors use the investment strategy of purchasing common stocks of companies with relatively low price-to-earnings (P/E) ratios and relatively high dividend yields. For example, they may favor companies that have a dividend yield well over the average for the stock market and a price/earnings ratio well under the average for the stock market. The logic behind this is that the stock price is depressed (a low P/E ratio), and hence the stock is being purchased when no one else wants it. This is in itself a good strategy so long as the company has no major long-term problems. This is what value investing is all about.

The dividend yield of such stocks is also attractive, and what

---

Table 7-1

Investing in Dividend-Paying Stocks for Increasing Income

DIVIDENDS DECLARED PER SHARE

Year	Coca-Cola	General Electric	Merck	Procter & Gamble
1985	$.12	$ .56	$ .18	$ .65
1986	.13	.59	.21	.66
1987	.14	.67	.27	.68
1988	.15	.73	.43	.69
1989	.17	.85	.55	.75
1990	.20	.96	.64	.88
1991	.24	1.04	.77	.98
1992	.28	1.16	.92	1.03
1993	.34	1.31	1.03	1.10
1994	.39	1.49	1.14	1.24
1995	.44	1.69	1.24	1.40

---

you're doing is betting that when the P/E ratio returns to normal, the company will increase its dividend to maintain an attractive dividend yield. If this happens, it's a win-win situation—your stock rises in value and your dividend payments increase.

• **Participate in dividend reinvestment plans.** If you own stock in one of the many corporations that offer dividend reinvestment plans, participating in the plan is a very smart way to add to your holding. Why? First, the company will either waive or sharply reduce any commissions incurred when reinvesting your dividends or when making an optional additional purchase of stock that you can make simply by sending a check to the company. Second, many companies also offer to sell you these additional shares at a slight discount. All in all, dividend reinvestment is a very convenient way to build up your stock investments. You generally have to take possession of the shares, rather than leaving them with your broker in order to participate in the dividend reinvestment plan. Some brokerage firms, however, are beginning to permit dividend reinvestment inside the brokerage account at a small additional charge.

The benefits go beyond building your portfolio at a minimum cost. Reinvestment is also a way for investors to force themselves to save. Rather than your receiving a small dividend check each quarter and then frittering the money away, the corporation automatically reinvests the money for you. Of course, if you are investing for income, dividend reinvesting may not be for you, since you'll stop receiving the dividend checks. One other drawback: You have to pay income taxes on the reinvested dividends as if you had received and cashed them in yourself.

Late breaking news: There's another trend that you should be aware of. A steadily increasing number of corporations are not only offering dividend reinvestment plans, but they will also sell shares directly to the public at no commission—free investing! (With a typical dividend reinvestment plan, your initial share purchases must be made through a broker.)

• **Be a long-term investor.** Finally, the buy-and-hold strategy of investing in stocks is almost always the best way to invest because the general market gains ground over time, and thus the value of most holdings increases. Only the most experienced investors who can devote a lot of time to their stocks are consistently successful with a "trading" strategy— one that involves frequent buying and selling. Studies have shown that over most holding periods of ten years or longer, buy-and-hold investors have enjoyed returns well in excess of inflation. Active traders generally have not fared as well. I realize that most investors go through a period of time when they're trading a lot. They probably think they can make a lot of money, but soon find out that they've actually lost some money—and hopefully have gained some wisdom from their folly. Simply put, active trading does not work for part-time investors.

Investing in Bonds

Buying bonds can be a daunting experience for the novice. You also have a good chance at paying more than you should, particularly for municipal and corporate bonds. The reason for this is that there are no published prices for munis and most corporate bonds so you're at the mercy of the bond salesperson. That's why it's crucial to be able to trust the firm and the person selling you the bond. It's not that you're going to be cheated in most instances, it's just that you may end up paying more for the bond than you should, which lowers your return—sometimes considerably. Moreover, you're going to need to rely on your broker or investment adviser to explain objectively the nuances of bond investing because there are a lot more suggestions and strategies for investing in bonds than I have space to offer here. That said, here are some recommendations and strategies that will help you become a successful bond investor.

• **Buy bonds when you think interest rates are high.** When you buy a bond, you are locking yourself into receiving a fixed amount of interest each year until the bond matures. If interest rates are quite low, it doesn't make a lot of sense to buy bonds, or if you do, you should only buy short-term bonds, in other words, bonds that mature within a few years.

How do you know when interest rates are attractive? That's always a tough call, but one rule you may want to think about is that if interest rates are considerably higher than the rate of inflation, particularly after the taxes you pay on the bond interest are considered, then interest rates are attractive. Another way of looking at it is to consider the interest rate currently being paid on the bellwether thirty-year Treasury bond. Bond pros suggest that if the rate on the thirty-year Treasury bond is near or over 7 percent, and inflation is well below that—say under 4 percent—then bonds should be pretty attractive. By the way, that doesn't mean you should buy a thirty-year Treasury bond. But interest rates across all maturity levels and across all types of bonds tend to move up or down as the yield on the thirty-year Treasury moves up or down.

• **Ladder maturities.** Smart investors do what is known as "laddering" or "staggering" the maturities of their bonds. Rather than investing in a single bond or in several bonds with roughly the same maturity, you should opt for a variety of maturities—some short-term (maturing in less than three years), some intermediate-term (three to ten years), and some long-term (maturing in over ten years). That way, if there is a significant change in interest rates, you will have avoided placing a heavy, and perhaps incorrect, bet on a single maturity. Laddering maturities reduces the risk of bonds. Don't forget to time some of the maturities to coincide with occasions when you may need the money—for instance to meet college tuition bills or to cover living expenses during your first few years of retirement.

Another word of caution. The longer the maturity of a bond, the more risk there is in that bond since you are locking yourself into a fixed rate of interest for many, many years. Therefore, a lot of savvy investors will invest exclusively or almost exclusively in short- and intermediate-term bonds. If they invest in long-term bonds at all, they typically don't go beyond a fifteen-year maturity. The additional interest you receive on long-term-maturity bonds in most interest-rate environments simply isn't worth the added risk. For example, the 7.5 percent that you receive on a twenty-five-year bond may seem more attractive than the 7.0 percent that you would receive on a twelve-year bond, but you're taking on a lot more risk by going with a longer maturity bond. Of course, in those rare instances where interest rates skyrocket you may want to take a chance by purchasing long-term bonds with some of your money. Say the yield on the thirty-year Treasury goes over 10 percent. Then you may want to snatch up some long-term bonds as long as you're convinced inflation won't stay high for many years hence. But 10 percent interest on high-quality bonds is a rare occurrence. In most cases, therefore, don't bet heavily on long-maturity bonds.

• **Beware of callable bonds.** Most municipal and corporate bonds can be called, that means retired, by the issuing corporation before maturity. U.S. Treasury securities are not callable, however. When investing in bonds, you have to be very careful about call provisions since bonds will often be called, if they can be, after interest rates have declined. Calling a bond allows the issuer to reissue the bonds at a lower interest rate. That certainly doesn't do you any good since you will then be confronted with having to reinvest your money in bonds that pay a lower interest rate since interest rates have declined. So whenever you are shopping for a municipal or corporate bond, be sure to ask about the bond issue's call provisions. Also, ask the broker to quote you the "yield to call," which is a measure of the interest that will be paid on the bond if the bond is called at the first call opportunity. If that amount is considerably less than the bond's "yield to maturity," ask your broker for a better bond. Careful shopping can usually locate issues that offer sufficient call protection.

• **Compare interest rates.** Yields (that's a fancy term for the effective interest rate the bond pays) vary among various types of bonds, both within the same investment category and between alternative categories. The same goes for all interest-earning securities. For example, chances are that the CD rate paid on CDs at your local bank is not as good as it might be if you shopped around a little. Another example: Over the past several years, interest rates on tax-exempt bonds have been very attractive compared with the after-tax returns on Treasury bonds and corporate bonds.

What is the lesson here? It pays to shop around for the best yields on your bond investments, just as it pays to shop around for other financial products and services that you need to achieve your financial dreams.

• **Consider the tax effect.** You will probably be able to increase your investment returns by carefully comparing the tax effects of alternative bond investments. Of course, you should do this within the context of maintaining a well-balanced portfolio as described in Chapter 2. But the way bonds are taxed can vary considerably. Some, like corporate bonds, are fully taxable; Treasury bonds are fully taxable but exempt from state taxes, and municipal bonds are usually exempt from federal, and perhaps state taxes. It's important to keep in mind that the most heavily taxed (and usually higher yielding) securities should be placed in your tax-deferred retirement accounts. On the other hand, tax-favored investments like municipal bonds should be placed in your taxable investments accounts and, if you reside in a state that assesses high taxes on investment income, your Treasury bond investments may be better placed in your taxable investment accounts as well.

Pay particular attention to municipal bonds because their return may well be higher than what you'd receive from a taxable bond after taxes are taken out. (For guidance on comparing municipal bond yields with taxable bond yields, see pages 63–65.)

• **Don't chase yield.** While shopping for yield is a virtue, chasing yield is a vice. A bond that pays 12 percent interest when prevailing rates are 7 percent is trying to tell you something. This is a junk bond or a close relative. Yet many investors erroneously think that the higher the yield, the more attractive the investment. This is not so. The higher the yield, the higher the risk. As many junk bond junkies have found out to their dismay, some of these bonds go down the tubes. While it may be appropriate to allocate a very small portion of your portfolio to more speculative bonds, be sure not to bet the ranch on them. In fact, if you take a fancy to junk bonds, by all means let the pros decide what to buy for you by investing in a high-yield bond.

• **Emphasize quality.** When you're having to buy individual bonds at around $10,000 a whack, it's difficult to achieve a lot of diversification unless you have a tremendous amount of money to invest. Therefore, you should buy primarily high-quality bonds. Treasury notes and bonds are considered the highest quality, so you should have no concern there. But with municipal and corporate bonds, quality varies, and you should not dip any lower than so-called "investment grade" municipal and corporate bonds. That usually means sticking with bonds that are rated "A" or better by Moody's and/or Standard & Poor's.

• **Buy only bonds that you expect to hold until maturity.** There are a lot of sophisticated players in the bond market who acquire bonds with the expectation of holding them only a short period of time—certainly not until they mature. Don't you be one of them. The individual investor has no place speculating on interest rate changes. True, it's possible to make a quick killing on a bond if you buy the bond and interest rates drop significantly soon thereafter. But before you sell, ask yourself what you're going to do with the proceeds. For example, perhaps you have a 7 percent bond and now interest rates are 5 percent. Yes, you can sell and make a nice capital gain on the bond, but what will you do with the proceeds? It doesn't make a whole lot of sense to sell a 7 percent bond, pay taxes on the profit, and then reinvest the money at 5 percent. It makes the most sense to buy a bond with every expectation of holding it until maturity. If you have to or want to sell it in the interim, so be it, but don't buy the bond in the first place expecting to do that. Another reason why you don't want to sell a bond is that if you think you get nicked a bit when you buy a bond, chances are you'll get scalped when you try to sell the bond because there aren't a whole lot of people out there who want to buy small denominations of bonds. Some dealers think a small denomination is anything under $1 million. So you'll probably pay someone dearly to do you the favor of buying back your bond.

- **Know your broker.** As mentioned earlier, some bonds are easier to purchase than others. You pretty much know how much you should be charged when you buy a Treasury note or bond or a listed corporate bond since their prices are published in the financial newspapers. But beyond that—with most corporate bonds and all municipal bonds—you have no idea what the market price is. You have to rely on the person who is selling you the bond to give you a reasonable deal. That's why it's crucial to know and trust the person who is selling you the bond. He or she should offer you a variety of alternatives based upon your investment requirements—risk rating and maturity. The bond should also have reasonable call protection. If you want to invest successfully in bonds, it's essential to have a good broker who will go to bat for you to find good bonds and negotiate a satisfactory price with the bond dealers.

Incidentally, if you want to get into buying Treasury notes and bonds, you should consider saving some money by buying them directly from the Treasury. Call your nearest Federal Reserve bank or branch (they should be listed under the U.S. government listings in the phone book) and request some information on their "Treasury Direct" program.

It's Up to You

If, after reading this section, you have concluded that buying individual bonds may be a wee bit too complicated for you, don't despair. Buying bonds successfully is tougher than buying stocks, no question. And there are a number of pros in this business who go so far as to suggest that individual investors should avoid buying municipal bonds and most corporate bonds in small denominations. Instead, they suggest restricting your municipal and corporate investments to mutual funds. I respect their opinions. On the other hand, there are a lot of investors who don't have a king's ransom and who enjoy buying individual bonds as much as they enjoy buying individual stocks, and they've done quite well with both. But it's up to you. And if you conclude at this juncture that buying individual bonds is not your cup of tea, don't despair. Bond funds are a more than acceptable alternative.

How You Can Profit from Options

Most investors buy call or put options on individual stocks because they think that the price of the stock will move significantly in one direction or the other. If you are right, you can make a much greater profit from an option than you could by buying the stock itself. The problem is that most investors, particularly part-time investors like you and me, can't predict these things accurately. In fact, the vast majority of all options on individual stocks expire worthless, resulting in a net loss to the option's buyer—and a net gain to that option's seller. Therein lies an opportunity that I'll describe shortly. So it would seem that buying stock options is best suited to investors who don't mind losing their money. That's because options are highly speculative investments. Unfortunately, many otherwise intelligent people succumb to the temptation of playing the options markets. However, there are a couple of ways where options may actually be of some benefit to you, but before telling you how, let's first look briefly at how options work.

How Options Work

While there are many different types of options, they usually fall into one of two categories: calls and puts. Buying a *call option* gives you the right—but not the obligation—to purchase 100 shares of a particular stock at a predetermined price at any time during the life of the option. Investors buy call options if they think the price of the stock is going to rise. Buying a *put option* gives you the right—

but not the obligation—to sell 100 shares of a particular stock at a specified price at any time during the life of the option. Put options are bought in anticipation of a falling stock price.

Every option has an *exercise price,* or *strike price.* This is the price at which you may exercise the right you obtained when you bought the option. Every option also has an expiration date, which is the last day on which the buyer is entitled to exercise the option to buy or sell the stock (usually the third Friday of a specified month).

Options are not written on all issues of common stock, only the most popular ones. Options are also traded on various stock indexes, such as the Standard & Poor's 500 stock index. Options are also available on foreign currencies, U.S. Treasury securities, and just about any other thing Wall Street can conjure up. Hardly a week goes by without an introduction of some newfangled type of option.

Two Sensible Ways to Use Options

1. Writing call options on stock you already own. Since the majority of option *buyers* end up losing money, it stands to reason that the majority of option writers (those who are willing to sell the options to the buyers) stand to make money. Therefore, you may want to consider writing covered call options—that is, writing options against stock that you now own—if options are available on the stock. Some investors find this to be an attractive, low-risk way to increase their investment income. Since you're writing options against stock you already own, the worst that could happen is that you would have to give up your stock at a price that will probably be lower than its market value if and when the stock is called away from you. But if you're careful writing covered call options, you'll probably end up with your stock intact and pocketing the money from the poor sap who bought your options. A couple of suggestions: Ask your broker to explain the nuances of covered call option writing and to help you set up a covered call writing program. Also, be sure to anticipate the worst—having to give up the stock—before you write options against it. Be particularly mindful of the capital gains taxes that you may incur if the stock is called away from you.

Warning: Writing options against stock you don't own (this is called writing uncovered or "naked" options) is one of the riskiest investment ventures in the history of mankind. You could lose everything you own—and then some—in a matter of minutes.

2. Buying put options on stocks that you think will decline in value. Put options allow you to make money if the price of a stock falls in value. So if you have a hunch that a stock is going to fall, you might want to buy a put option on that stock. Buying put options can be used in lieu of selling the stock short. Short-selling is a risky technique where you profit if a stock declines in value. When you sell a stock short, you actually sell stock that you don't own and then later complete the process by buying the stock. If the stock has fallen in value, you make money. Doesn't this sound illegal or unethical? Well, it isn't. But, if you sell a stock short, and it subsequently rises in price, your risk of loss is—theoretically, at least—unlimited. On the other hand, the most you can lose with a put option is the amount you paid for it. So a major advantage of puts over selling short is that the risks are known and limited.

Here are two other ways to use options that can make sense for some investors, but I'm not going to go into the details:

• Protect a gain or contain a potential loss in a stock that you hold but don't want to sell.

• Protect all or a portion of your investments from a decline in stock prices by using options on a stock index, such as the S&P 500.

If you want to get into these or other sophisticated options strategies, you should first do some homework and then work only with a trustworthy broker. Never fall for the options pitches that some unscrupulous people may pitch to you.

IPOs—More Sizzle Than Steak

Initial Public Offerings (IPOs) are new issues of stock in companies that were previously privately held. Issuing stock gives the company a valuable new source of capital as well as a listing on a stock exchange. Most IPOs come out when the stock market is very strong. After all, wouldn't you want to sell something when there are hoards of buyers eagerly awaiting your product? But while there is opportunity to make money with IPOs, there is also a lot of risk. And unfortunately, the benefits inure to the firms that assemble the IPOs and a few *lucky* individuals who get the stock at the initial offering price. I hate to be blunt about this, but you're probably not one of those few who can profit mightily from an IPO. Unless you're a major client of your broker, chances are that when you receive a call inviting you to get in on this once-in-a-lifetime opportunity, the particular IPO you're offered is not going to be one of the better ones. The good ones are snapped up by the insiders and big-time investors.

On the other hand, some IPOs offer wonderful potential, and they could be a very respectable investment. But you must take the time to review the company's financial data, including the information that is contained in the company's prospectus. Many IPOs are nothing but smoke and mirrors—yet investors flock to them like ducks to a Junebug. Don't you be one of them. But if the stock is something that makes sense to you, you can certainly contact your broker to see if you can get any shares. That's probably a long shot. Alternatively, you can always buy the stock just after it has gone public, but I would caution you to steer clear if the price has risen substantially. Otherwise, you could be setting yourself up for a disappointing downhill ride. All too often, hot IPOs end up cooling off after the big shots have made their money and the little guys jump in. Here's the sad chronology.

The Sad Chronology of a Hot IPO

- Insiders and big-time investors get most of the new shares.
- Stock goes public and price skyrockets.
- Insiders and big-time investors sell their holdings at a great profit to eager, but naïve investors.
- Stock price plummets shortly thereafter.
- Average investors are left to wonder how such a hot stock could manage to lose so much money in such a short period of time.

CHAPTER 8

The End of the Road—Deciding When to Sell a Stock or Bond

Thoughtful investors often agonize whenever they *purchase* a stock or bond. Deciding when to sell a stock or bond is often an even tougher decision. Perhaps that's why most investors don't do a very good job of it. Every investor in stocks and bonds has occasionally sold a good investment too soon or failed to get out of lousy investment soon enough. That's life. But you also don't want to make a habit of it. Here, then, are some suggestions for deciding when to sell a stock or a bond.

Figuring Out When to Sell a Stock

Knowing which stocks in your portfolio to sell, and when to sell them, is at least as important as knowing when to buy a stock. One rule that is elusive to most investors is that any stock you now hold that you don't currently consider to be an attractive "buy" candidate should be considered a candidate for sale. Of course, potential capital gains or losses must be taken into consideration. But you don't want to hold on to a stock if it doesn't have attractive future prospects. And for heaven's sake don't hold on to a stock for sentimental reasons. If you really feel obligated to honor Aunt Nell's or Grandpa Harry's memory by holding on to a particular stock that doesn't look too hot right now, you can prudently honor their memory by holding on to just *one share.*

Warning Signs

There are several red flags that should alert you to the potential need to sell stock.

- If the company's growth rate or earnings trend peaks and then falls, selling should be considered.
- If a company cuts its dividend or ceases to pay a dividend, it is usually a sign that the company is in trouble.
- Stock market experts even go so far as to say that if a dividend remains steady or if its rate of increase is behind that of the market in general, it may be time to sell.
- Price targets are another means of hedging against drops in the market. Here, investors establish predetermined low and high price targets from which they depart only under extreme circumstances. If the share price goes below its low price target, it probably should be sold.
- When a stock reaches the predetermined upper limit, it may also be time to sell unless new information warrants holding on for further potential gain. But realizing profits now may be better than waiting for an additional gain, which may not materialize.

General Market Guidelines

While the most important time to sell a stock is when its future prospects are deteriorating, you may also want to lighten up on stocks if it appears that the overall market is going to decline. No matter how good your stock is, if the overall market declines, your stocks are also probably going to decline as well. Here are some general guidelines for predicting market declines, although, of course, the direction of the stock market can never be consistently predicted. The following indicators may signal that the market is headed for a drop. Most of the information to which they refer is easily obtainable in the financial pages of the newspaper.

- Rising interest rates can divert money from stocks to competing investments, thereby depressing stock prices.
- Historically, recessions have often been preceded by stock market declines. Therefore, early indications of an economic slump may be reason to decrease market exposure somewhat. On the other hand, stock prices have often rebounded before the end of a recession, which argues against selling stocks during a recession.
- Soaring stock prices that lead to high price/earnings ratios and depressed dividend yields are often signs that market prices are unsustainable.

See Chapter 12 for more guidance on unfriendly investment markets.

Guidelines for Selling

Although there are no foolproof methods for selling stocks (or buying stocks for that matter), the following suggestions and guidelines should be considered.

Haste Makes Waste Don't buy a stock with the intention of selling it soon thereafter. One of the reasons you should be buying high-quality stocks is to avoid having to worry all the time about whether or not you should sell them. Most often, when you buy a stock you should feel that it is an investment that you will want to hold on to indefinitely.

Two-Year Rule   Here's one rule that you might want to consider: If you own a stock that fails to keep up with the Standard & Poor's 500 Stock Average over two consecutive years, then you should consider selling it. This tactic may mean that you hold on to a poor investment longer than you should, but that mistake is often better than selling too soon. Unless something negative happens to the company, stick with it for a while.

Stop-Loss Orders   Using a stop-loss order can protect gains or limit losses. With stop-loss orders, you give your broker instructions to sell if a particular stock's price drops to a certain point. Stop-loss orders can be useful and economical for investors because they can be placed through their broker free of charge and can limit losses to whatever amount their portfolios can accept. These orders can be made for a limited period of time or be good until canceled. They are especially popular when the market trend is downward or when an investor is uncertain about a particular stock. Unfortunately, stop-loss orders cannot be placed on all stocks.

Before you put stop-loss orders on all your stocks, you need to understand that there is some risk in doing so. First, you should guard against "whipsawing"—the possibility that the price of the stock may fall low enough to force a sale and then rise again after you have been closed out of your position. This occurs most often when the stop-loss order is placed too close to the current market price. On the other hand, if the stop-loss order is placed too far from the market, it no longer protects against dramatic losses. I recommend that you generally place your stop-loss order price at a level of 15 to 20 percent below the current market price of the stock to prevent the possibility of being whipsawed.

Tax Timing You should also evaluate the timing of a sale of stock in light of the taxes that will be paid on the capital gain—or the capital loss that will be incurred if you sell at a loss. For example, there may be situations in which it is beneficial for you to defer capital gains until the following year. Or, you may want to sell a stock at a loss late in the year to offset capital gains you have earned on other investments during the year.

It's Often Not an Either/Or Decision Investors who are contemplating selling a stock usually think that the decision is either to sell all the position or to hold on to it. That's not what the professional investors do, however. Unless they are absolutely certain that this stock is going to fall out of bed— and that certainly doesn't occur very often—the pros will sell half of the position and then defer making a decision on the other half. That way, if the stock rebounds, they've still got a position in it. On the other hand, if their fears end up being realized and the stock declines, their exposure to that stock is less than if they had done nothing and held on to all of it.

Selling Bonds—If You Have To

Selling a bond before it matures is a decision that should not be taken lightly. First, as I indicated in Chapter 7, you shouldn't buy a bond unless you intend to hold it until it matures. Nevertheless, there may be situations where either you have to sell the bond to raise cash or it makes good financial sense to sell the bond. One major and compelling reason why you might want to sell a bond is if the financial condition of the issuer—a corporation or municipality—is deteriorating. But, unless it's a Treasury bond or listed corporate bond, you are at the mercy of the bond dealers, who probably don't want to be bothered if the bond you want to sell is quite small. Incidentally, what a bond dealer considers to be "quite small" is huge to most individual investors. So you will probably pay dearly for the privilege of selling your bond. Here is where a reliable broker can be very helpful, not only in getting a fair price for the bond when you want to sell but also in keeping you apprised of any changes in the credit status of bonds that you hold. Another important role your broker can play is to advise you about which of the bonds you own are the best candidates for sale.

Finally, your broker may recommend "bond swaps," particularly if you have losses in some of the bonds you own because interest rates have been rising. A bond swap may allow you to realize a capital loss on the bond you sell while picking up some additional yield by swapping into an equivalent or better bond. Bond swaps can be very beneficial if, as is usually but not always the case, your best interests are your broker's foremost consideration.

PART III

Actively Managing Your Investment Portfolio—An Hour a Month Can Add Thousands of Dollars to Your Investments Each Year

CHAPTER 9

Where to Find Useful
Investment Information

By following my four easy steps to investing, you can be a successful investor. But you can improve your investment results by spending some time reading, listening to, or watching the many sources of good information on every facet of investing. The abundant and ever-growing sources of reliable information are good news to anyone who wants to spend some time taking advantage of them. The bad news is that there is so much mediocre and downright bad information, that the task of separating the bad from the good can seem overwhelming. In this chapter, I will help you identify and use investment information effectively and efficiently. In the following chapter, I will discuss using the computer to help you invest more successfully.

There are hundreds of information sources, including newspapers, newsletters, and investor services; books, almanacs, and magazines; television and radio programs; and educational courses.

What Type of Information Do You Need?

To decide where to look for investment information, you must first decide what type of information you need and what information formats are most convenient to you.

For example, new investors may benefit from community education programs to learn about investing. For the "intermediate" investor primarily interested in mutual funds, there are mutual fund monitoring services, magazines, newspaper columns, and newsletters that cover mutual funds. For more experienced investors, there are numerous sources that cover the overall investment climate and individual stocks and bonds. Finally, investors who work well with computers can enjoy a growing number of computer programs and easily accessible databases that give you up-to-the-minute facts and analyses. If you have access to a computer, you will definitely want to read the next chapter.

Newpapers

The quintessential newspaper for the business and financial community is *The Wall Street Journal,* which devotes a whole section each weekday to money and investing. It is, and has for generations, been *the* place to turn for up-to-date investment news and analysis and price quotations. Serious investors also swear by *Barron's,* a business and financial weekly that provides more analytical financial articles and a statistical section without peer. It comes out on Saturday mornings and true investment junkies will spend most of the day pouring over its pages.

In addition, there is *Investor's Business Daily,* which, as its name implies, is geared more toward investors. *Investor's Business Daily* provides more detailed stock information and financial charts than the *Wall Street Journal,* which services a wider audience. The above publications are joined by a slew of other investment newspapers and newspaper columns, and the quality of these is usually quite good.

Magazines

Magazines such as *Business Week, Forbes, Fortune,* and *The Economist* cover both business and investing. The two topics blend easily together, since business news is generally used for investing. All of the magazines have timely articles and columns on the investment markets.

If you want less business news and more general information on investing, money management, and related topics be sure to check out *Kiplinger's Personal Finance, Money, Smart Money, Worth,* and *Your Money.* I like all of these magazines, although I'm not about to rely on any single one's recommendation of a specific investment. Rather, I take their recommendations and do a little bit of research myself.

Newsletters

Those who seek a publication that provides a specific investment focus may want to subscribe to one of the hundreds of investment newsletters. They come in all shapes and colors. Some focus on stocks or bonds; others deal entirely with mutual funds. Many provide specific investment recommendations, along with the type of financial information you'd expect to get from a Wall Street insider.

While newsletters can be a useful source of investment ideas, I strongly encourage you not to rely on the specific investment suggestions or strategies proffered by a single newsletter writer (no matter how accurate the author claims to have been). Most newsletters that provide specific investment recommendations have a mediocre track record. A number use ranking systems, models, or some other supposedly sophisticated mathematical approach to predicting financial trends and investment picks. But sophistication doesn't guarantee success—some would argue it does the opposite. One important matter to keep in mind when considering the recommendations of investment newsletters is that they often justify their existence by recommending frequent trading in your account, while most investors are better off by adopting a buy-and-hold strategy.   .

Investor Services

If you want to delve into detailed information on the investment markets in general or particular investments, there are some respected investor services that offer a wealth of detailed financial news. Their names have become synonymous with no-nonsense investment information. But these services cost a lot, so you should probably use them at your local library.

Moody's Investor Service doesn't just provide bond ratings. It supplies publications for professional and nonprofessional investors alike, including several manuals that give detailed financial and descriptive information on numerous companies. Standard & Poor's Corporation also is an excellent source of financial information. S&P *Stock Reports* provides a lot of historical and current performance information for thousands of stocks. S&P also publishes the quarterly *Stock Market Encyclopedia* and the monthly *Stock Guide*, which tracks the performance of more than 5,000 stocks.

Value Line publishes the highly respected *Value Line Investment Survey*, as well as a variety of other important publications. The *Value Line Investment Survey* regularly evaluates over 1,700 stocks. Many investors who buy individual stocks swear by Value Line and are willing to pay over $500 per year for a subscription. If this would put too much of a dent in your wallet, chances are your local library subscribes to the service.

Mutual Fund Monitoring Services

In addition to numerous mutual fund newsletters, as well as extensive coverage in newspapers and magazines, you can receive timely information on individual mutual funds by referring to one of the major mutual fund monitoring services. Two widely respected services, *Morningstar* and the *Value Line Mutual Fund Survey* provide up-to-date data and rankings for most stock and bond mutual funds. In addition, both provide detailed descriptions of each fund. These services are a great way to evaluate and select mutual funds. Many active fund investors subscribe to one or both of these publications, which are available in print or on computer disk. Others seek them out in their local libraries.

If you use either of these services, be sure to refer to the guidebooks that accompany each that explain the information provided for each fund. That way, you can make the most of these wonderful resources.

Television and Radio Programs

Investing and financial planning is a popular topic for just about every adult. In fact, studies have shown that American adults spend more time thinking about money than any other subject! The television and radio industry has responded by offering an ever-increasing amount of coverage on these topics. Some of the cable networks offer extensive daily coverage of the investment markets. Public television offers three nationally broadcast programs, including *Nightly Business Report*, a daily television program that offers an in-depth review of daily market action, business news, interviews, and commentary. (Yours truly serves as the financial planning and mutual fund commentator on *Nightly Business Report*.) The other two PBS productions are the weekly *Adam Smith's Money World* which looks at a variety of industry topics that would be of interest to active investors and the venerable *Wall Street Week with Louis Rukeyser*. This weekly program assembles several very knowledgeable individuals in the investment business, including a weekly special guest to chat about the market.

Radio commentary and financial talk shows abound, offering up investment opinion, recommendations, and education. Many of the talk shows answer listener questions on the air and can be very informative. Be forewarned, however, that the hosts of many local radio financial programs actually pay the station for the privilege of hosting the program. While that doesn't necessarily mean you won't get good information, the host is obviously trying to tout his own services; otherwise, why would he pay to appear?

Educational Courses

Night courses and weekend seminars can be a useful way to tap the knowledge and experience of someone who works in the investment field. If you are relatively new to investing, or desire a refresher course, it can help to have a live person explaining financial concepts. More experienced investors may benefit from seminars that provide more focused information and the opportunity to talk over ideas.

If you take one of these courses, you should be aware that many individuals who teach education courses or conduct seminars want to sell you something, and usually it's themselves. Financial planners, stockbrokers, and insurance agents often teach these courses for purposes of attracting new clients—and may therefore be biased toward specific investment products.

There is nothing wrong with being wanted as a client. One advantage, in fact, to taking a course from financial merchants is that because these individuals are practicing their craft, the discussion is likely to be practical, not theoretical. Also, you have a chance to view the person's investment approach and knowledge without being obligated to do business with him or her.

Investment Clubs

Another great way to learn about investing is to join an investment club. These clubs use a team approach to selecting investments. An investment club is a group of individuals who meet once a month, contribute a set dollar amount, and invest the common pool of money in stocks. Every member is responsible for doing research on individual stocks on a rotating basis. They then report their findings to the club, and members debate the risks and rewards of each stock and finally take a vote on which ones to buy. I'm not surprised that a lot of these clubs end up beating the market pros with their stock selections.

Much of the guidance for these clubs comes from the National Association of Investors Corporation (NAIC), a nonprofit organization. For details on joining a club, contact them at 810-583-6242.

When Looking for Investment Information, Don't Forget the Mutual Fund Companies and Brokerage Firms

Many investors don't realize it, but the mutual fund companies and brokerage firms they do business with publish prodigious amounts of helpful information for their customers. Most full-service brokerage firms have a bevy of analysts who produce reports on particular companies, industries, and even the economy in general. These reports are available from your broker for the asking.

Mutual fund companies publish a variety of very helpful educational brochures for investors. Many of them also offer software products—either free or at low cost—that will help you plan your investing. Most no-load companies will gladly send you their publications even if you don't have an account with them. Just call their 800 numbers and ask.

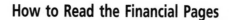

How to Read the Financial Pages

Over the years the financial community has developed a shorthand system for providing financial information. In a brief column giving cryptic abbreviations and numbers, the cognoscenti learn the story of how a particular investment has been doing. Fortunately, if you are not already among the cognoscenti, it's easy to be. The following is primer for reading the stock, mutual fund, and bond listings in your newspaper. However, the newspaper you use may not include all of this information in its quotations.

Mutual Funds

As the importance of mutual funds has grown, the availability of mutual fund quotations has increased. Now that *The Wall Street Journal* and many other newspapers publish mutual fund quotations every day, investors are able to get a fix on how their fund, or prospective fund investments are doing. The Friday edition of *The Wall Street Journal* includes very comprehensive performance data and rankings of mutual funds.

Information included varies from newspaper to newspaper, but the following are among the most common categories of information.

Inv. Obj.   This abbreviation describes the investment goals of a fund as stated in its prospectus. GI, for example, may indicate that a fund's objective is growth and income.

NAV   NAV stands for net asset value—the price of a share of the fund at the previous day's market close.

Offer price   This term indicates what you would pay per share were you to purchase shares in the fund. Offer price represents the net asset value plus sales commissions, if any.

In addition, the following quotation footnotes often will appear directly after the name of the fund:

p   This letter indicates that the fund charges a 12b-1 fee (that's an additional annual charge that some funds assess to help cover marketing and distribution costs).

r   This letter indicates that the fund may charge a redemption fee. A redemption fee is a charge levied by some funds when the investor eventually sells the fund's shares.

t   This letter indicates that the fund charges both a 12b-1 and a redemption fee.

NL or n   This abbreviation indicates that no sales load or contingent deferred sales load is charged. A sales load is a charge that is assessed when the fund is purchased. A contingent deferred sales load or charge is assessed if an investor sells the fund's shares within a few years after buying them.

x   This letter stands for ex-dividend, which means that new share buyers will not receive the fund's next dividend payout.

Total return, YTD   Some newspapers will list performance calculations since the beginning of January as percentages, assuming reinvestment of all dividend and capital gains distributions. (YTD means year-to-date.) Sales charges, if any, are not reflected. In addition, performance calculations for different periods of time—the last year, for example—may also be included.

It's important to note that a fund can either have a *p* or an *r* symbol listed next to it and still be called a no-load fund. However, a fund with a *t* can't be so listed.

Stocks

Stock prices on the New York and American exchanges and the Nasdaq Stock Market are tracked using the system described below.

52 Weeks Hi/Lo   Gives the highest and lowest price per share of the stock during the past fifty-two weeks.

Stock   This term provides the name of the company issuing the stock.

Sym   This abbreviation indicates the stock's trading symbol.

Div   This abbreviation is used to provide the latest annual dividend per share paid by the stock.

Yld   This abbreviation provides the stock's latest annual dividend expressed as a percentage of the stock's price on that day.

PE   This term gives the price/earnings ratio (the price of a stock divided by the issuing company's past year's earnings per share).

Hi/Lo/Close   This term expresses the stock's volatility in terms of a single share's price movements. The *Hi* shows the top price for a single share during a trading day. The *Lo* shows the lowest price for a single share during a trading day. The *Close* is what the price of the stock will open at on the next trading day.

Net Chg   This abbreviation indicates by how much the price of an individual share rose or fell during a particular day.

s or x   These symbols may appear in the left-hand column. An *s* indicates that the stock has split or the company issued a stock dividend within the last year. An *x* stands for "ex-dividend," meaning the new investors won't receive the next dividend.

Bonds

Bond quotations are presented in a variety of formats because there are many types of bonds. Some of the most common abbreviations within these listings include the following:

Issue   This term indicates the issuer's name.

Coupon   This term provides the interest rate at which the bond was issued.

Mat   This abbreviation indicates the month and year in which the bond matures.

Price   This term gives the price at which the bond closed. For example, a price of 98 3/4 means a bond closed at 98 3/4 percent per $1,000 of par value, or at $987.50.

Chg This abbreviation reflects the increase or decrease in the price of a bond as compared with its previous day's closing.

YTM This abbreviation indicates the bond's yield to maturity.

CV This abbreviation indicates the issue is a convertible bond; i.e., it can be exchanged for a fixed number of shares of common stock from the issuer.

CHAPTER 10

—— ∞ ——

Using the Computer to Monitor Your Portfolio

The rapid development of the cyberspace and on-line investing are among the biggest changes in the securities and investment industry of the twentieth century. Investors can choose among hundreds of software packages to automate almost any of their investing chores. There is software that helps you determine your investment strategy, select a balanced portfolio, and track its progress; software that gives individual investors unprecedented access to up-to-the-minute, company-specific information or industry reports along with databases with historical information on thousands of securities; software with the ability to perform sophisticated analyses; software that lets you make electronic trades.

So no longer are individual investors dependent on stock tips from their brokers. Through the information superhighway, they now have easy access to all kinds of investment-related information once reserved for big institutional investors. Low-cost trades can be placed with the touch of a finger. In an industry where information is king, the cyberspace market-place offers many advantages to investors who are willing to spend a little time investigating what's available.

So you've got a computer and are interested in how your computer may be able to help you be a better investor. Where do you go from here? I'm going to give you an overview of how you can use your computer, where you can get more information, and some general guidelines you should keep in mind.

The Information Superhighway

Cyberspace Wall Street is a giant marketplace, including commercial on-line services, financial newswires and publishers, on-line brokers, analytical and database software by financial institutions, and much, much more.

Commercial On-line Services

If you are not already among the millions of subscribers to one of the commercial on-line services, this could be a good place to start if you don't want to fling yourself directly into the internet. On the plus side, these services offer user support and features the whole family can use in addition to varying levels of investment-related information. On the minus side, their databases are limited; they screen fewer fields than the top CD-ROM and disk-based software. If you use them a lot, they can be expensive. So watch your charges.

Investment-related information, including financial and economic news, investment analysis, and market data, can be gathered through the commercial on-line service powerhouses. Targeting the needs of individual investors, they offer market and portfolio updates as part of their basic services. They also provide some company fundamental research (including company news and balance sheets, earnings reports, and stock ratings and analysis).

Offerings are changing and improving all the time, particularly now that these commercial services are facing increasingly stiff competition from the internet. To compare them for ease of use as well as for content, take advantage of free trial periods before committing to one or more commercial on-line services.

Worldwide Web

The internet's worldwide web is a huge global network consisting of a large collection of multimedia sites containing information and links to other sites. There are literally thousands of investment information related sites offered by leading financial institutions—and some not-so-leading financial institutions. InvestSIG is one of the best web sites for investors. It provides access to a wide range of information sources such as market news, stock quotes, historical data, mutual fund information, investment journals, articles, and newsletters. Other top web sites focus on investments, finance, and economics, and they include major university-based web sites.

While the list is expanding constantly, here's what's on the internet for investors.

- Investment letters
- Business and financial newspapers
- Electronic magazines
- Clipping services
- Specialty newswires
- Quotes and market index reports
- Company analysis
- Industry and research analysis
- SEC filings
- Investment discussion clubs
- Mutual fund analysis

- Information on stock indexes, options, and futures
- Commodities and futures trading information
- Technical analysis
- Foreign investments

Getting on the Internet

To get on the internet, you'll need an internet service provider (ISP), either a big national one or a local ISP. Costs can vary considerably, depending on whether you can get a local access phone number and on how many services are covered by the basic monthly fee. Most charge one-time fees to install their software, but a national ISP is generally the least costly route to the internet if you are going to be using it more than about ten hours a month. To keep your monthly cost to a minimum, your provider's software should include e-mail, a file transfer protocol for downloading files, a web browser, and free technical support. Increasingly, there are deals to be had as competition intensifies. Once you have a web browser, you can take advantage of these powerful search tools to gain access to the internet's vast database containing documents from millions of web sites.

What's Available On-line?
Information, Information, Information

Hardly a day goes by without some additional nugget of investment information becoming available on-line. Here is just a sampling.

Financial Publications   Most mainstream financial newspapers and magazines and many smaller, more specialized publications have gone on-line. One of the biggest advantages of the electronic newspapers is that they act almost like newswire services: Unlike the traditional print newspaper, stories on the electronic newspapers are updated continuously around the clock.

Mutual Fund Companies and Brokerage Firms Mutual fund companies and brokerage firms have also joined the cyberspace race. Many financial institutions have created web sites to provide a variety of information on mutual funds and other investments. Most of the fund company web sites let you read and/or download fund prospectuses or order them electronically. Some also provide information and advice on investment and retirement planning, including investment allocation worksheets to help you determine your risk tolerance and investment time horizon and design a portfolio accordingly. In the end, as expected, you are steered toward the particular company's funds or other investments, but I guess we can forgive them for that.

Newswire Services Parallel to the mass-market-oriented commercial on-line services, there are big information players providing high-powered services primarily for institutional investors. These giant players, including Dow Jones, Reuters, and Bloomberg, offer vast coverage of financial news, market data, and powerful analytical tools. But, alas, most come at a high price, which could be anywhere from $1,000 to $2,500 per month. As the smaller investor's demand for investment information has grown, however, the big players have begun to take this market more seriously and are developing low-cost alternatives. They are now providing some services on-line to small investors, often through one of the commercial on-line services or independently at a small monthly charge.

Securities Evaluation and Portfolio Management Software

There are hundreds of powerful software tools that could help you become a better investor. First, let's look at the kinds of programs that are useful to just about every investor. *Investment allocation* software can help you refine the mix of investment categories that will best meet your unique investment requirements, taking into consideration such things as your tolerance for risk, your need for liquidity, and your need for current income. *Fundamental analysis* software can identify and screen stocks or mutual funds that meet your basic investment requirements, using information from disks updated weekly, monthly, or quarterly, or from on-line databases. *Technical analysis* software shows you hundreds of different indicators you can use to try to identify major trends in individual securities or in the stock market as a whole. *Bond analysis* software lets you project bonds returns under various interest rate scenarios. And *portfolio management* software makes periodic updates from electronic databases to monitor the performance of your investments and keep you abreast of your portfolio's value as well as alerting you to possible danger signs. Basic portfolio management software will also track commissions, profits, and taxes and prepare graphs and reports.

Most of the major personal finance software programs also have basic investment allocation and portfolio management capabilities that may be enough for your needs. So do the commercial on-line services. But before you buy any program or sign up for any service, think about whether your portfolio is likely to grow more complicated in the next year or two, and consider the inconvenience (not to mention the error potential) of transferring all your data from one program to another if you outgrow the capabilities of the first. You may decide that you might as well start out with a more powerful portfolio management package that supports transactions and includes both fundamental and technical analysis programs.

There's a downside to buying a high-end software package with multiple, integrated capabilities though. It's likely to have a long, steep learning curve. This means that you'll need to consider not only the initial cost of the software, but the added cost of books to supplement inadequate manuals, and courses to supplement inadequate books, before you'll be able to learn how to use all the features. You should also factor in the cost of accessing the databases you'll need to use. Some are free on the internet; many are not. The commercial on-line services may attach surcharges to many of the sections you'll want to use. And disk services have an annual fee attached. The greatest cost of all may well be your time. So consider what your time is worth as you weigh the benefits of a souped-up software package against the cost.

The internet also offers a variety of freeware and shareware, but think twice before you download. Almost anything goes, and there's virtually no accountability. You have no way of knowing for sure what the software does, or how many bugs it has (or its viral potential, a different kind of and far more dangerous bug). Technical support for freeware and shareware is likely to be marginal and/or expensive, and compatibility problems with other software are almost a given. "Free" may not be such a great deal, at least in the area of financial software.

On-Line Trading

The rapid development of the information superhighway has empowered individual investors, and with the rising power of individual investors, more trading volume has been shifted onto the new cyberspace Wall Street. It won't be too long before most brokerage firms, including the nation's largest discounters, will be allowing their millions of customers to trade stocks and mutual funds on-line.

To establish a new link with electronic brokers, you need to open an account with the firm and acquire its proprietary software. So long as you have a personal computer and a modem, you're in business. Most brokers also offer ways to let their customers make securities transactions on-line through the world wide web or one of the commercial on-line services. Trading on-line is just as easy as sending an e-mail message: Once you have signed on and linked to your broker, input the stock symbol, number of shares, specify whether you are placing a market order or limit order, and click "okay." In a moment, you will get a trade confirmation from the broker.

In addition to on-line trading services, most brokers now offer trading related bundles of products and services in one-stop packages. These include statistical and analytic software and portfolio management software designed to meet just about all investors' needs. One such package provides instant access to real-time quotes, massive historical and current data, securities and mutual funds screening capacities, portfolio monitoring capabilities, graphing and analytic tools, and third-party products. Whew! The third-party products offered by brokers often include high-powered research tools. Most of them, though, come at extra cost. In a way, the electronic brokers are becoming "full-service discount brokers on the cyberspace."

But perhaps the biggest advantage of investing on-line is lower trading expenses—a 10 percent or greater discount is typical. The deepest discount on-line brokers charge minimum commissions as low as $12 per trade—and competition may lower them even further. Another advantage is that orders can be completed twenty-four hours a day. Orders placed during off-hours can be executed during the next day's trading hours, after the investor verifies the current stock price.

On-line trading is becoming an increasingly popular option for individual investors. As more advanced technologies continue shifting financial power to you and me, even more rapid expansion of on-line trading is expected in the future. In effect, a new generation of empowered cyberspace investors is transforming one of the country's oldest industries.

Should you join the ranks of on-line traders? In my opinion, if you make your own investment decisions, you should buy and sell securities in whatever way gives you the lowest transaction costs, and most discount brokers now offer on-line trading services. Electronic trading is not without its perils, however. One is technical, another psychological. First, make sure you use what's called "secure aware" software when you are making a trade or giving a broker personal portfolio information. Second, make sure every trade fits your long-term investment strategy. Trading on-line is easy and fast. Beware of the temptation to trade too often. It doesn't work.

For Up-to-Date Information

You can use your computer to make a simple capital gains tax calculation, identify and screen potential investments, perform sophisticated analyses, trade on-line, or exchange information with other individual investors about everything from software to a specific company's management problems. And the possibilities are expanding daily. One of the world wide web's strengths is its unregulated, unplanned, continuous chaotic growth. That's also what makes it daunting to beginners. Your best bet, if you want to get started but are wondering how you'll ever make sense of it, is to look over one of the growing number of directories/navigators explaining the internet's "structure" and maybe pick up a copy of a Web Yellow Pages covering the business and finance sites. Check your library or bookstore.

The biggest problem you will face if and when you decide to use the computer to help you invest is deciding what services to use. Not only are the number of services overwhelming, but new and improved products and services are being introduced at a ferocious pace.

One good way to find current information is by perusing some of the mainstream computer publications such as *PC Computing, PC Magazine, PC World, Windows Magazine, Macworld,* or *Information Week.* Other resources include *Individual Investor, Investor's Software Review,* and *Wall Street Software Digest.* The Chicago-based American Association of

Individual Investors puts out an annual paperback, *Guide to Computerized Investing*, plus a monthly newsletter. And if you have access to the internet, you can ask questions about specific software in a forum or Usenet newsgroup and get the scoop from other investors who already use it. (Just make sure you don't get a vendor's sales pitch disguised as a testimonial from a user.)

What's the Bottom Line?

I know too many people who feel compelled to use all available computer resources just because they're now so easy to access. They are afraid that if they're selective, they'll miss something. So their time disappears as they sit glued to their monitors and the resulting information overload creates analysis paralysis. What's even worse—at least for the health of a long-term portfolio—is that their new awareness of the hourly ups and downs of their investments sometimes creates so much anxiety that they are driven to respond with actions that go directly against their own investment strategies—and good sense.

The individual investor can find a wealth of computer resources. You can certainly benefit if you take the time to decide what you need and use your information wisely. And you can lose your shirt if you are not alert to scams, unsubstantiated information, or the potentially addictive charms of real-time trading. No matter what programs or services you select, always remember that computers and computer software are just tools—not an investment adviser. Use your computer to collect and analyze data and generate reports, but trade on not only the information you gather from the computer but also on your own good judgment.

Overall, the best advice I can offer is the same advice I've given you on making investment decisions *without* using the computer: Don't act on anything you don't understand.

CHAPTER 11

---⊗⊗⊗---

Ten Ways to Minimize
Taxes on Your Investments

Income taxes on dividends, interest, and capital gains can take a tremendous whack out of your investment income. Successful investors will strive to beat inflation on their investments by 3 percent *after taxes have been taken out.* Of course, you can't do this every year. Some years it is easy to achieve this investment objective; in years when the stock and bond markets are down, it's impossible. But over the long run, if your after-tax returns can handily beat inflation, you are well on your way to achieving your financial dreams—and once you've achieved them you will be able to maintain them for the rest of your life.

Of course, allocating your investments appropriately and spending some time selecting worthwhile investments are crucial to achieving this goal. But another way to make sure you are making the most of your investment returns is always to be aware of the tax effects of any investment you will make. By paying attention to taxes, you can *dramatically* increase your investment returns. In fact, tax-wise investing strategies are one of the best ways to win at the investing game. Unfortunately, many people fail to pay sufficient attention to taxes. That's a shame, because it's really not difficult to become a tax-savvy investor.

TAXES CAN TURN AN ATTRACTIVE INVESTMENT RETURN INTO A MEDIOCRE RETURN. Do you know how much of a bite taxes take out of your investment earnings? For most investors, capital gains are taxed at 28 percent by Uncle Sam and may well be subject to state capital gains taxes. With state taxes factored in, it's not unusual for you to be giving up one-third of your capital gains. Even if Congress gets around to lowering the capital gains rate, taxes will still be a big impediment to achieving decent returns. Most investors pay at least 28 percent federal income taxes on dividend and interest income. High-income taxpayers pay even more. Add state income taxes to that, and investors are giving back to the government anywhere from one-third to almost one-half of their dividend and interest income.

I am always amused—and bemused—at how little attention people pay to the effect of income taxes. Someone with a salary of $50,000 probably thinks he makes $50,000, but he doesn't. He probably makes—or takes home—closer to $40,000. So it is with investments. You might hear someone say, "I got a pretty good deal on a CD last week. I'm getting six percent." Well, unless the CD is in a retirement account, that investor is making nowhere near 6 percent. If federal and state income taxes eat up one-third, she's really only making 4 percent on the CD. (Here's the math: 6 percent × ⅓ = 2 percent in taxes; 6 percent interest - 2 percent taxes = 4 percent after taxes.) Now, if inflation is chugging along at 3½ percent, our friend with the 6 percent CD who forgets about taxes probably thinks she's doing pretty well. After all, she surmises she is beating inflation by 2½ percent. But that's *before taxes*. After taxes, she's only beating inflation by ½ percent. Now that's better than falling behind inflation, but if your portfolio only beats inflation by ½ percent, it's going to take you a lot longer to accumulate the money you need to achieve and maintain financial security than someone whose investments are providing a higher after-tax return.

There is quite a bit of discussion about tax-saving ideas throughout this book. Here is a summary of the ten most important tax-saving investment strategies.

1. Take Advantage of Retirement Plan Investing

One of the best ways to ensure that your investments beat inflation after taxes over the long term is to put them into investments that aren't taxed along the way, including tax-deferred (and usually tax-deductible) retirement accounts.

Tax-deferred retirement accounts include company retirement savings plans, self-employed retirement plans, IRAs, deferred annuities, etc. These beauties generally come with dual benefits: Most of the time the money you contribute to these plans is not subject to income taxes (two exceptions are deferred annuities, and for some people who participate in other retirement plans, IRA contributions are not deductible.) Second, in all instances, the income earned on the money you contribute is not taxed until you begin making withdrawals, usually when you're retired. But there is a catch. You cannot withdraw any of the money in a retirement account until you are at least age 59½ (there are some exceptions to this). That's a small price to pay for the wonderful tax advantages. So long as you know that you can afford to put the money away until retirement, you should take maximum advantage of any and all retirement savings plans that are available to you.

For more information on tax-advantaged investing, including which of the alternatives may be best for you, please take a look at Chapter 13.

2. Put Your Most Heavily Taxed Investments into Your Least Heavily Taxed Investment Accounts

Sound confusing? It isn't really. First, there are obvious things to avoid. For example, never put a municipal bond or a municipal bond mutual fund into a retirement account. It makes no sense to put a security whose income is tax exempt, or, in the case of a deferred annuity, whose income is tax deferred, into an account that is already tax advantaged.

But there are some less obvious strategies here that will enable you to reduce the tax bite on your investment income.

The following list shows investments that usually pass on a lot of taxable interest, dividends, and/or capital gains. The best place for these are your tax-deferred retirement accounts.

PUT THESE HEAVILY TAXED INVESTMENTS IN YOUR TAX-DEFERRED RETIREMENT PLAN ACCOUNTS

Most stock mutual funds[1]
Corporate bonds and corporate bond mutual funds
Zero-coupon U.S. Treasury bonds

The following list shows investments that are not subject to heavy income taxes or investments over which you have control of the timing of capital gains income. Since these investments have certain tax advantages, they should generally be put in your taxable investment accounts.

PUT THESE TAX-FAVORED INVESTMENTS IN YOUR TAXABLE INVESTMENT ACCOUNTS

Municipal bonds and municipal bond funds
Individual stocks

[1]Exceptions are so-called "tax-efficient funds," which as a matter of policy try to minimize the capital gains that are passed on to shareholders—index funds, for example.

Tax-efficient stock mutual funds, such as index funds

U.S. Treasury bonds and U.S. Treasury bond mutual funds (if you live in a state that imposes high state income taxes on interest income)

3. Always Compare After-Tax Returns on Bond Investments

Too many investors simply add bonds, bond mutual funds, or other interest-earning investments to their taxable accounts without considering the tax effects of each. Consider the following example.

> **EXAMPLE:** Henry Henderson is a happy investor. When ten-year Treasury bonds hit 6½ percent interest, Henry took advantage of the opportunity. He thought that kind of return was hard to beat. He could have bought a high-quality ten-year corporate bond for 7½ percent, but he'd have had to pay 6 percent state income tax on the interest. With this investment he won't pay any state taxes on the Treasury bonds. Municipal bonds with a ten-year maturity are paying just 5½ percent in his state. He couldn't see investing in something paying that puny rate of interest, so he took advantage of the Treasury bonds.

Henry should have done some homework. A few simple calculations would have shown that he would have been better off financially with either of the other choices. See Table 11–1.

The moral of the story here is always to consider income taxes whenever you make a bond investment. It's more difficult to compare bond mutual funds on an after-tax basis since the yields on bond funds will vary over time as the managers are constantly buying and selling bonds in the fund portfolio. But you can still compare the current yields offered by the

---
Table 11-1

It Pays to Compare Interest Rates

	U.S. TREASURY BOND	CORPORATE BOND	MUNICIPAL BOND
Interest rate	6.5%	7.5%	5.5%
Subtract income taxes:	[28% federal tax 28% × 6.5%]	[34% federal and state tax[1] × 7.5%]	[No federal or or state income taxes]
	(1.8%)	(2.5%)	0%
After-tax interest	4.7%	5.0%	5.5%

[1]28% federal and 6% state income tax rate

---

various bond fund categories when you are getting ready to buy a fund to see which offers you the best after-tax return.

4. Include Some Tax-Efficient Mutual Funds in Your Taxable Investment Accounts

Each year at tax time, mutual fund investors face some unpleasant surprises. Mutual fund companies are required to pass along their realized capital gains, interest, and dividends to their shareholders. Taxes can greatly reduce a fund's performance. Tax liabilities are rarely a concern of most fund managers whose role is to obtain the highest total (before tax) return, except when tax efficiency is among the fund's objectives. Therefore, it is up to you to choose funds that are right for your tax situation. Yet most investors pay little heed of this—to their financial detriment.

Of course, when you put a fund into a tax-deferred retirement account, taxes are of no immediate concern. It's when you put funds into a taxable investing account that taxes become a concern.

Tax Efficiency of Mutual Funds

The relative tax efficiency of a mutual fund depends largely upon the fund's investment objectives and the way in which it is managed. At one extreme, all or virtually all of the income distributed by single-state municipal money-market funds is not taxable. At the other end, funds striving for capital appreciation often distribute large capital gains to shareholders. And for funds that trade frequently, many of these capital gains could be short term, which equates into a capital-gains rate that is higher than 28 percent for investors who are in higher tax brackets. Between the two extremes are endless varieties in terms of tax efficiencies.

Funds that invest in municipal securities are the most tax efficient because of the federal and perhaps state exemption of muni interest income. Nevertheless, any realized capital gains earned by a muni fund—or any fund for that matter— are subject to tax.

With respect to stock funds, index funds, which employ a buy-and-hold strategy, are more tax efficient than actively managed funds. Research shows that actively managed funds need to achieve two to three percentage points higher in pre-tax annual returns than index funds to offset the tax liabilities resulting from active trading. Stock index funds have generally posted better after-tax returns than the average actively managed stock fund in recent years. For more information on index funds, see pages 40–43.

The investment style of a fund may also affect its shareholder's tax obligations. Lower turnover funds tend to have smaller capital-gains distributions than higher turnover funds. (Turnover is the measure of how frequently the fund manager buys and sells securities in the fund.) Growth funds usually have a relatively lower dividend distribution compared with income funds.

But within most stock fund categories, there are some funds that are intentionally managed to minimize taxes. These funds go one step further than index funds in their efforts to minimize tax liabilities. They may employ a number of strategies, including deliberately selling losers to offset gains from other stocks, selling shares with the highest tax cost basis when less than an entire position is sold, minimizing turnover, and avoiding high-yield stocks. Many of the larger mutual fund companies offer tax-efficient funds that use one or more of these strategies.

Minimizing Your Mutual Fund Tax Bill

Of course, you shouldn't let taxes override other considerations that are usually more important, including past investment performance and how a particular fund complements your other investment holdings. But taxes should receive at least some consideration when you select a mutual fund. After all, income taxes can easily consume one-third or more of your investment income. Anything that can be done to minimize that bite while still meeting your overall investment objectives merits your serious attention.

Always investigate before you invest. Two funds with similar stated performance figures may produce quite different after-tax returns. Here are some things to consider:

1. Before buying a bond or stock fund, find out what percentage of its total returns have been paid out as dividends and capital gains in recent years. Funds with lower taxable distributions tend to pay higher after-tax returns to their shareholders.
2. Turnover rate is another consideration. In general, the higher a fund's turnover rate—in other words, the more the manager buys and sells securities in the fund portfolio—the larger its short-term capital-gains distributions. Although two funds may have similar unrealized capital gains, the one with the lower turnover rate will probably take a longer time to distribute its gains. Mutual funds

have an average turnover rate of about 80 percent, but some have much lower rates—as low as 15 percent.

3. Another way to predict a fund's future tax liabilities is to find out how much unrealized capital appreciation is already built into the fund portfolio. The unrealized capital appreciation is a rough indicator of the fund's potential tax liability; in general, the higher the unrealized capital appreciation, the greater the future capital-gains distributions will be.

4. Finally, put those otherwise desirable funds that are the most tax "unfriendly" in an individual retirement account, company-sponsored retirement plan, variable annuity, or other tax-deferred investment account, and let them accumulate without your having to worry about paying taxes along the way.

Incidentally, the information about each of the fund tax matters that I discussed above can be obtained either by calling the mutual fund company or by referring to one of the mutual fund monitoring services at your library, notably *Morningstar* or the *Value Line Mutual Fund Survey*.

5. Buy Individual Stocks So That You Can Decide When to Pay Capital Gains Taxes

As I mentioned in Chapter 5, the way the rich get richer is by buying and holding individual stocks (or real estate), letting them appreciate in value throughout their lifetimes, and then passing them on to their heirs (even though they don't deserve them), who inherit the stocks not at the price their ancestors paid for them, but rather at the price of the stock when the dearly departed departed. Now, you might ask, these people must have been pretty rich if they didn't have to sell any stock along the way. Well, they lived off the dividends, which probably increased at a rate greater than inflation over the years. The beauty of individual stocks is that you aren't having to pay capital gains every year as you would with most stock mutual funds. In short, owning individual stocks is a very tax-wise way to invest.

6. Take Advantage of Your Child's Lower Tax Rate If You Are Investing for College

Chapter 15 discusses how to invest money destined to pay college tuition. One idea that will be raised, and bears pointing out here, is making sure that you take advantage of the lower tax rate enjoyed by youngsters. For children under fourteen, there are limits to the amount of investment income they can earn. If it exceeds that amount, they are taxed at the parents' tax rate. But there is usually no reason not to put enough college-earmarked money in the child's name to earn investment income up to the limit. Beginning at age fourteen, all income earned by a youngster will be taxed at the child's tax rate. As Table 11-2 shows, taking advantage of a child's lower income tax rate can save hundreds of dollars in taxes each year.

─────── **Table 11-2** ───────

The Advantage of Investing in Your Child's Name

	INVESTMENT IN PARENTS' NAME[1]	INVESTMENT IN CHILD'S NAME
Taxable investment income	$1,000	$1,000
Subtract income taxes	(330)	(100)
After-tax income	$670	$900

Tax savings by investing in child's name ($900 − $670) = $230

[1] Parents are assumed to be in the 33% federal and state tax bracket.

7. Compare Interest Rates on Short-Term Investments

While short-term investments are pretty mediocre in terms of the interest they pay, periodically comparing the interest paid on various short-term investments will help you tweak out some extra returns that, over the years, can really add up. See Chapter 17 to learn how to compare returns among the many types of low-risk short-term investments.

8. Keep Careful Records of Investments to Minimize Capital-Gains Taxes When You Sell

Whatever you invest in, you will be able to reduce your tax bill by keeping detailed records of purchases, sales, and reinvestments. Otherwise, when you are faced with having to establish the cost basis of investments that have been sold, daunted by the complexity of it all, you will likely take the easy way out and use a method (or guesstimate) that could lead to either overpaying taxes or facing an embarrassing meeting with the IRS.

There are limitations on the choice of methods that can be used to establish cost basis. Refer to any of the tax preparation guides for more details. Suffice it say, however, that the better the records you keep, the lower the taxes you will pay. And that's like money in the bank.

If your past tax records haven't been up to snuff, begin to maintain records of every stock, bond, and mutual fund transaction. Organize these records so that you understand the history of what has happened and file them where you know you'll find them when you need them.

9. When You're Retired, Delay Withdrawing Money from Retirement Accounts as Long as Possible

The vast majority of retirees should delay withdrawing money from retirement accounts for as long as possible. Of course, when you reach age seventy and a half you have to begin making at least minimum withdrawals. But the longer you can delay taking money out of these accounts, the more time they will have to continue growing tax-deferred. If you follow this usually wise strategy, you may even have to eat into some of the principal in your taxable investment accounts to help meet living expenses, but that's okay. Remember, when you withdraw principal that has already been taxed, there are no more taxes due on the money. In contrast, all or the vast majority of the money you withdraw from a retirement account will be taxable.

If you have a sizable amount of money in all of your retirement accounts—amounts approaching or over $1 million, you should speak with a tax or estate-planning expert to see if it makes sense to begin making withdrawals from your retirement accounts sooner than age seventy and a half or withdrawing more than the minimum required amounts after age seventy and a half—even if you don't need the money to meet living expenses. (The IRS has temporarily suspended imposition of the 15 percent excise tax in 1997 and 1998.) Otherwise, you may be subject to a 15 percent excise tax on some of the money withdrawn from large retirement plan accounts.

For more information on investing wisely when you're retired, please see Chapter 18.

10. Don't Lose Sight of Estate Taxes When Planning Your Investments Later in Life

Investment decisions that are made later in life can affect the amount of money that you pass on to your heirs. Consider the following situation.

EXAMPLE: Rather than pay a one-month's interest penalty on a six-month CD, John Johnson, age eighty-three, sold $10,000 worth of stock to help pay some living expenses. He'd held the stock for several years, having originally paid

$4,000 for it. He paid $2,000 in capital-gains taxes on the $6,000 capital gains, leaving him $8,0000 after taxes. Unfortunately, John was penny wise and pound foolish. He died shortly thereafter, leaving his heirs $2,000 less than he would have had he cashed in the $10,000 CD and paid a $50 interest penalty. By selling low-basis securities, he had to pay a capital gains tax that would have been avoided altogether had he passed on those low-basis securities.

The idea here is to avoid, where possible, any transactions late in life that result in capital-gains taxes that could be avoided altogether if the securities were kept intact and passed on to the next generation. An expert in tax and estate planning can help guide you through the complexities of coordinating your income taxes with your estate taxes. But investing some money in good professional advice could result in fewer dollars going to the taxing authorities and more dollars going to your heirs.

CHAPTER 12

⟨⟨⟨⟩⟩⟩

Oh No! Surviving a Market Decline

What would you do if the Dow Jones Industrial Average dropped 700 points next Monday? What would you do if Dr. Bear arrived at your doorstep, draining 25 percent from the value of your stocks slowly, ever so slowly, over the next two years? Or what would you do if interest rates skyrocketed, leaving your bonds and bond funds seriously wounded? Will any of these events ever happen? No one knows, of course. But if the past is any indicator, they probably will. In fact, the stock market has suffered corrections of 10 percent or more 106 times in this century—over once a year, on average. In fact, we've had twenty-nine corrections of 20 percent or more, roughly one every three years. While the unprecedented bull market during the 1980s and through the mid-1990s has led many investors to conclude that the market will rise forever, in fact stock market corrections, and steep ones at times, are inevitable.

How you react to these miserable investment experiences will play an important role in your long-term investment success. It's the investors who get frightened into making big changes in the way they invest that end up with mediocre investment results. People who exit the stock market to avoid a decline or amidst a decline are odds-on favorites to miss the next rally. If you were out of stocks in forty key months over the past forty years, your annual stock investment returns would have dropped from over 11 percent to 3 percent. Most of those key times when stocks rose mightily in a single month happened right after stocks took a dive.

People who hold back investing their money because they think stock prices are too high or stocks will soon go down in value also end up missing the boat. Since 1965, if you bought stocks once a year and were unlucky enough to pick the worst day to invest—the day when stocks were at their highest level for the year—and did so thirty years in a row, you ended up with an annual return of 10.6 percent. If you were incredibly lucky and invested on the best day of the year thirty years in a row, you would have ended up with an annual return of 11.7 percent, so the difference between perfect timing and horrendous timing is a mere 1.1 percent.

Coping with Investment Losses

Many investors overreact to unexpected market downturns. Of course, market downturns are always unexpected. No one rings a bell on Wall Street to tell investors that stocks are going to decline. The really jittery types are inclined to and may in fact dump all their long-term investments and retreat to the safety of low-yield, short-term investments like money market accounts. Lest you be tempted to do the same, here are some guidelines that will help you to continue to invest successfully even when the financial world seems on the verge of collapse or seems to be in the midst of collapse.

- **When in doubt, doing nothing is often best.** Many investors react too suddenly to adverse market conditions, and they almost always do the wrong thing. In fact, selling when one should be holding, if not buying, is an almost surefire way to lose money. As uncomfortable as it may seem at the time, doing nothing may be the best way to react during a crisis. In general, you should never "sell into market weakness." Wait until things settle down. Also, be very wary of the immediate opinions of experts amidst and right after the crisis. Ask yourself: "If they're such experts, why didn't they predict this mess in the first place?"

• **Diversify.** Once again, it pays to follow this most basic and time-honored investment truism. All too many people have too much money invested in the stock of one or a very few companies, in a single mutual fund category, or in real estate, or in long-term bonds. This can be a recipe for disaster if the particular investment sector on which you are concentrating falters badly. The better diversified you are, the better position you will be in to emerge from the scary market relatively unscathed.

• **Always remember that you are investing for the long term.** The 500-point, single-day drop in the Dow Jones Industrial Average on October 19, 1987, did not provoke another Great Depression. Indeed, the total decline during the 1987 market erased only one year's gain in the Dow. (The Dow Jones average actually ended 1987 with an overall gain, not a loss.) Flat, if not down twelve-month stock markets aren't that uncommon, yet few people remembered this fact during the 1987 postcrash hysteria. Investing for the long term—a principle equal in importance to diversifying—will usually give you greater rewards on your investments and a better night's sleep.

If You Must Do Something . . .

It may be too much to ask to simply sit by idly when the market has just suddenly dropped or is in the process of declining slowly. You may feel that you must do something, and if it will help you sleep better at night, here are some defensive measures you can take without jeopardizing your sound long-term investment program.

• **Emphasize quality investments.** True, the market is driven by rumors and unfounded fears. True, short-term changes in stock and bond prices often have little to do with companies' underlying values or financial health. But stocks of quality, dividend-paying companies, and bonds of financially sound issuers—and mutual funds that invest in these securities—will have more staying power if market conditions do continue to deteriorate.

One way to fine-tune your investments without falling into the trap of making a major shift in your investment allocation is to prune out lower quality securities (or funds that invest in such securities) and replace them with higher quality securities and funds. If you follow my investment allocation recommendations in Chapter 2, your portfolio will already be protected because my allocations emphasize higher quality securities.

• **Opt for mutual funds that do well in bear markets.** If the market turns against investors, there is nothing that is going to prevent mutual funds from suffering a decline. But some mutual fund managers are better able to cope with unfriendly markets. In other words, they don't lose as much. How do you identify these funds? The mutual fund monitoring services (see page 101) report the performance of each fund in both up and down markets. You might want to shift some of your money into funds that have proven themselves to be particularly adept at coping with past unfavorable market conditions.

• **Use stop-loss orders on stocks.** A stop-loss order, which instructs your broker to sell a stock if it declines below a level that you specify, will help protect your stocks against sharp and/or rapid market drops. Unfortunately, you may find that the broker can't put stop-loss orders on all of your stocks.

Remember also that they are not foolproof. In a fluctuating market, for example, you may be sold out of stock that subsequently rebounds in price; therefore, you usually want to set your stop-loss price at a level considerably below the current market price for your stock—at least 15 percent below.

• **Reduce your margin borrowing.** The investors who are really hurt by sharp market downturns are those who invest "on margin"—they use borrowed money to invest. If stock prices drop, the brokerage firm may require the investor to add more cash to the account. So the only way for most investors to cover their "margin calls" is to sell some of their stock holdings at a most inopportune time. While margin investing can be an effective means for very experienced investors to increase the returns on an investment portfolio, heavily margined investors expose themselves to considerable risk. If you are heavily margined and are concerned about market conditions, do the prudent thing and reduce your margin now rather than being forced to reduce your margin later.

• **Emphasize short-maturity bonds and bond funds.** If your bond investments are falling in value, that means interest rates are rising. The longer the maturity of your bond or bond mutual fund, the more the value of that investment reacts to changing interest rates. One way to reduce the fluctuation in bond and bond fund values when interest rates are rising is to emphasize short-term bonds and bond funds. Like all sensible strategies in lousy market conditions, this won't prevent you from losing money, but you will end up losing a lot less money than you would if you had stuck with long-term bonds and long-term bond funds.

• **Emphasize defensive investing strategies.** You will hear a lot about "defensive investing" when stock or bond market conditions are particularly worrisome. Defensive investing emphasizes avoiding serious losses by concentrating on investments that are thought to be resistant to significant loss. When investment market conditions are unusually uncertain or adverse, many investors prefer defensive investments.

Chances are that your mutual fund managers are doing the same with the money you have in their funds.

Defensive stock groups listed below should, but won't necessarily, perform better than other groups during a rocky economy. (Note that these groups produce goods and services that we use under any economic conditions.) A defensive investment is one made primarily to protect yourself against declining stock prices. In the stock arena, defensive investors opt for high-quality stocks in so-called "defensive" industries. This does not mean investing in weapons manufacturers.

- Beverages
- Cosmetics
- Drugs
- Foods
- Health care

- Liquor
- Supermarkets
- Telephones
- Tobacco
- Utilities

A defensive bond investment strategy involves an emphasis on high-quality bonds—typically U.S. Treasury securities or corporate and municipal bonds that are highly rated by the rating agencies, namely Standard & Poor's and Moody's. Defensive investors also may prefer short-maturity bonds and bond funds that, as discussed above, will fluctuate in value less than long-maturity bonds in response to changes in interest rates.

- **Make moderate changes in your investment allocation.** If market conditions are particularly bad or if you really fear that the stock market is headed for disaster, I could abide your making *minor* modifications to your overall investment allocation. I emphasize *minor* modifications because if you start to make major shifts in investments, you are, in effect, timing the market. And I hope by now that you know market timing doesn't work. At any point, there are a bevy of Wall Street experts who are predicting disaster. Disaster in the investment markets is a relatively rare occurrence. If you follow the advice of these self-proclaimed experts, you are simply headed for trouble.

So here's one approach if you feel compelled to lighten up on stocks. You could change your investment allocation strategy as described in Chapter 1 from:

- Aggressive to moderate, if your current allocation is aggressive
- Moderate to conservative, if your current allocation is moderate

If your current allocation is conservative, I wouldn't make any changes—you are already invested conservatively enough.

Incidentally, while you may think these are minor modifications to your investment allocation in the face of adverse market conditions, I consider them rather drastic. Chances are your fears are unfounded. But your real problem will be deciding when to go back to your original investment allocation approach. It may be easy to lighten up on stocks when you are scared, but it's a really tough task deciding when to get back in. Here's how bad it can get: I had a caller on a radio talk show in mid-1996 who asked me if I thought it was all right for him to get back into the stock market. He said that he had become frightened of stocks and got out of the stock market entirely and has been in a quandary ever since trying to decide when to get back in. I asked him when he got out of stocks. He replied, "Just after the 1987 market crash." Stocks have more than tripled since this poor chap abandoned stocks. Imagine how he feels as he struggles now to figure out when to get back in. Sad but true for too many investors. Don't let fear get in the way of sensible investing.

PART IV

Special Situations

CHAPTER 13

───— ◇◇◇◇ ───—

Choosing the Best Retirement
Savings Plan and
Tax-Advantaged Investments

Do you know how badly taxes on interest, dividends, and capital gains can erode your investment returns? As explained in Chapter 11, taxes can easily turn what appears to be an attractive investment return into a mediocre one at best. In fact, what may appear at first glance to be an inflation-beating return ends up losing ground to inflation after Uncle Sam has taken his piece of the action.

But there are ways to keep all of what you earn, at least temporarily. All retirement accounts and some individual investments are tax-advantaged. Tax-advantaged retirement accounts and individual investments fall under one of three categories, as Table 13-1 shows.

Some Tax-Advantaged Investments
Are Better Than Others

Choosing the best tax-advantaged investments can be confusing. But, depending upon your own circumstances, some tax-

---

Table 13-1

Types of Tax-Advantaged Investments

	CONTRIBUTIONS	INVESTMENT EARNINGS	EXAMPLES
DEDUCTIBLE TAX-DEFERRED	Deductible	Tax-deferred until withdrawal	• 401 (k) • 403 (b) • SIMPLE • SEP • Keogh • Deductible IRA
NONDEDUCTIBLE TAX-DEFERRED	Not deductible	Tax-deferred until withdrawn or sold	• Nondeductible IRA • Individual stock and real estate investments • Deferred annuity
TAX-FREE	Not deductible	Interest is tax-exempt; capital gains are taxable	• Municipal bond • Municipal bond mutual fund

---

advantaged investments are superior to others. In general, any tax-advantaged investment that permits you to contribute tax-deductible dollars is where your money should go first. But after you have maxed out on all tax-deductible retirement plan investments, you'll still probably want and need to contribute to other tax-advantaged investments. This is when the situation gets more complicated. Table 13-2 should help you identify those tax-advantaged investment accounts and investments that are best for you based upon your employment status. If any of these terms are confusing to you, check the following glossary.

Tax-Advantaged Investment Glossary

Deductible Tax-Deferred Investments

401(k) Plan   Among the most attractive tax-advantaged retirement investment accounts your money can buy are 401(k)s. When you participate in a 401(k) plan, your employer diverts a fixed portion of your pretax salary into a company-sponsored investment plan. There are two advantages to this: Your overall taxable income amount is reduced, which is the equivalent of a tax-deductible contribution, and, as with all tax-deferred investments, your money grows tax-deferred until you begin withdrawing it when you're retired. Many employers match part of each employee's contribution to 401(k)s, which is icing on the cake.

403(b) Plan   If you work for an educational institution, government, or other nonprofit organization you may be eligible to participate in a 403(b) plan. Also known as *tax-sheltered annuities,* 403(b)s are a special type of salary-reduction retirement savings plans that are similar to 401(k)s. And they have the same advantages of 401(k)s insofar as the money that you contribute to the plan is not subject to federal income taxes, and your contributions grow tax-deferred until they are withdrawn. Other similar plans are also available at various nonprofit organizations.

SIMPLE Plan   SIMPLE stands for Savings Incentive Match Plan for Employees. Certain small businesses can set up SIMPLE retirement plans for their employees. As with the 401(k) or 403(b) plan, employees elect to have contributions deducted from their pay.

Table 13-2

The Best Tax-Advantaged Investments for You

CHECK YOUR STATUS:

☐ I am an employee	☐ I am self-employed	☐ I am an employee but I also have some self-employment income	☐ I am retired or have no job income

HERE ARE YOUR BEST TAX-ADVANTAGED INVESTMENTS:

BEST	401(k),SIMPLE, or 403(b), if available from your employer	SEP or Keogh plan	401(k), SIMPLE, or 403(b), if available from your employer	Delay withdrawing retirement plan investment (IRAs, etc.) as long as possible.
SECOND BEST	IRA	IRA	SEP or Keogh plan	Buying and holding individual stocks and real estate
THIRD BEST	Buying and holding individual stocks and real estate	Buying and holding individual stocks and real estate	IRA	Municipal bonds and bond funds
ALSO WORTH CONSIDERING	• Deferred annuities • Municipal bonds and municipal bond funds	• Deferred annuities • Municipal bonds and municipal bond funds	• Buying and holding individual stocks and real estate • Deferred annuities • Municipal bonds and bond funds	

SEP Plan A SEP is a Simplified Employee Pension Plan that is simple to set up, simple to maintain, and a simply wonderful way for self-employed people to save for retirement. Instead of maintaining a separate pension plan (required with a Keogh plan, which is described below), you simply complete a simple IRS form (Form 5305-SEP, to be exact) to set up the SEP. Then, each year you take the SEP contributions out of your business's checking account and deposit them into your (and, if applicable, your employees') IRA accounts. Your contributions to a SEP are tax-deductible.

Keogh Plan A Keogh plan is a formal arrangement in which a self-employed person (but not a corporation) establishes a retirement plan for the owner(s) and their eligible employees, if any. As with SEP plans, Keoghs permit self-employed people to set aside a considerable amount of money each year. All contributions to the account are tax-deductible, and all investment earnings in the account accumulate tax-free until withdrawn.

Tax-Deductible IRA There are two types of IRA contributions—tax-deductible (discussed now) and nondeductible (discussed below). If neither you nor your spouse is an active participant in a qualified retirement plan, you may make tax-deductible IRA contributions regardless of your income. Fully or partially tax-deductible IRAs are also available if you participate in company retirement plans but your adjusted gross income is below $25,000 for a single taxpayer or $50,000 for married taxpayers. Deductible IRAs are simply too attractive to pass up. Think of it this way: If you are in the 28 percent federal tax bracket you can either contribute $2,000 into a tax-deferred retirement account or you can pay an extra $560 in income taxes ($2,000 in extra taxable income × 28 percent). Spouses who don't work outside the home can also contribute up to $2,000 per year to an IRA, beginning in 1997.

Nondeductible Tax-Deferred Investments

Nondeductible IRA   If you are not eligible for a deductible IRA, you should still consider the advantages of a nondeductible IRA as a place to put money that you can afford to part with until retirement. Nondeductible IRAs still provide the benefits of tax-deferral on all income earned in the IRA account.

Holding Individual Stock and/or Real Estate   While many people don't think of it in these terms, buying and holding individual stocks (not stock funds) and real estate are in and of themselves tax-deferred investments. Why? Because so long as you hold on to the stock or the property, you pay no taxes on its appreciation in value until you sell it. Many of the families who have accumulated a lot of wealth in this country have done so by buying and holding stock and/or real estate. These rich folks enjoy a rising source of dividend and rental income (which is taxable), but they never pay a dime of tax on the appreciation in value of their stock and real estate investments until they sell them.

Deferred Annuity   A deferred annuity is an investment account that is used to accumulate retirement savings. While the money you put into a deferred annuity is not tax deductible, your investment capital grows tax deferred. Many investors are attracted to the tax-deferral benefits of deferred annuities, which, unlike other tax-advantaged retirement accounts, have no limit in the amount you can contribute. But wise savers will not contribute to a deferred annuity until they have taken advantage of all other retirement savings accounts that are at least somewhat more attractive than are deferred annuities, largely because these other accounts are less expensive to maintain.

Tax-Free Investments

Municipal Bonds and Municipal Bond Mutual Funds You don't have to be rich to benefit from tax-free investing. Interest earned on most municipal bonds and municipal bond mutual funds is not subject to federal income taxes. If you own a bond issued by a municipality or state agency in your home state or if you purchase a single-state municipal bond mutual fund that restricts its investments to municipal bond issuers in your state, you enjoy interest income that is free from both state and federal income taxes. While municipal bonds usually don't pay as much interest as Treasury or corporate bonds, after taxes have been taken into consideration, municipals have pretty consistently provided a higher after-tax return than have taxable bonds. Remember, it's what's left over after the tax people have been paid that's most important.

CHAPTER 14

~~~

Does Real Estate Belong in Your Investment Portfolio?

It sure does. Real estate has been one of the best ways for people of average means to build their wealth. There's a special feeling about owning property, and about having other people paying *you*. But as many real estate investors in the late 1980s and early 1990s learned, it is also possible to lose a great deal of money in the real estate market. Some people lost their life's savings because when the real estate market was hot, they wanted to get into real estate in a bad way—and when the market turned cold they found that they actually *did* get into real estate in a bad way. Like all good investments, real estate can be risky.

Does the prospect of being a landlord appeal to you? If your answer is a resounding "no," there are ways to own real estate that require no more effort to manage than a few strokes of a pen to write out a check to pay for the investment.

I'll start by discussing own-it-yourself real estate because that's the best way to make money in real estate. Then, I'll examine a couple of other ways to participate in real estate investing without the hassle of property management.

Own It Yourself

Buying individual properties is the best way to own real estate. It provides the greatest potential returns and is how a lot of wealthy families in this country got wealthy. That said, owning it yourself is the riskiest way to get into real estate. It's your neck that's on the line and no one else's. And it's also not for those who don't want to deal with pesky tenants.

The best way to start is to begin small. Make sure you genuinely are cut out to be a landlord and to deal with the sometimes vexing details involving tenants and property. Also, don't become overextended with debt—which would result in disaster the next time a downturn occurs as vacancies rise and property prices drops.

What Type of Property?

There are a whole range of different types of income-producing properties available to you. But some are clearly better than others, as I will explain below.

Residential Rental Property A residential rental property can be anything from a single-family home to a large apartment building. Location, condition, and occupancy rates will all affect the property's value, as can local and neighborhood population trends and zoning changes. As you probably know, the most important consideration in any real estate parcel is location. This truism is particularly crucial to residential real estate. While a few savvy real estate investors have been able to benefit by taking early stakes in "turnaround neighborhoods" this sort of gambling is best left to the professional.

SINGLE-FAMILY HOMES AND CONDOMINIUMS. These are often the first investments that come to mind for new real estate investors, but they almost always make lousy real estate investments. The reason is very simple. It is difficult to find properties that are priced low enough that the rental income is sufficient to cover mortgage and operating expenses. You'll soon tire of pumping money into a property that is not self-supporting. And if you invest in such a property, you are in essence placing a heavy bet that the property will appreciate smartly and soon. That's a big gamble.

You may also think that a vacation home constitutes a real estate investment. Vacation homes may be a great source of relaxation, but they're usually poor investments. People who buy a vacation home as an investment have their heads in the beach sand. They probably believe the breathless assertions of the real estate salespeople that it will have great rent potential. Sure, you may be lucky enough to rent it for $1,000 a week, but did the broker tell you that the peak rental season lasts only two weeks? And those are the two weeks when you want to use the place? Or people who buy vacation time shares— the quintessential bad investment—probably believe they can actually swap their time share on the Canadian border for an oceanfront place in Monte Carlo. Don't get me wrong, there may be a very good reason to buy a vacation home, mainly for enjoyment, but don't be deluded into thinking it will be a good investment. You'll be a lot better off renting a place instead. The owners will be very grateful for getting some cash out of their vacation albatrosses.

MULTIFAMILY HOMES AND APARTMENTS. There are much greater opportunities for success with multifamily apartments than with single-family homes and condos. Included in this category are small two-, three-, and four-family homes that are often owner-occupied. In fact, if you want to purchase your own home and get into the rental real estate game, you can accomplish both at the same time by buying a small apartment building—a duplex or a triplex.

Multifamily dwellings require a greater initial investment but the cost per dwelling unit is lower, so the investment makes much greater investment sense. Multifamily units are relatively easy to finance if you have sufficient money to make the down payment, since lenders see the potential rental income as protection on their loans.

Commercial Property   Office buildings, shopping centers, and industrial real estate all offer investors with substantial resources an opportunity for significant gains, albeit at significant risk. But with the exception of very small, well-located, and fully occupied properties, commercial real estate is best left to the experts.

How to Evaluate an Investment

Suppose you come across a small apartment that really appeals to you? It is in good condition, has some architectural character, and seems to be located in an up-and-coming neighborhood. While all these factors may make you want to buy the property, they are meaningless until you know what it costs to operate the building and how much income it generates. Once you have these figures in hand—and have a good idea of the property's selling price—you can then determine whether buying it makes any sense. The following yardsticks for evaluating real estate investments will help you make just that decision.

Rent Multiplier   The simplest way to evaluate whether a property is attractively priced is to compare the price you'd have to pay for it with its current gross annual rental. Any property selling for much more than seven or eight times the gross annual rental is likely to yield a negative cash flow—in other words, your rental income won't be sufficient to cover your mortgage and operating expenses, let alone make a profit. To determine the rent multiplier, which compares the total selling price with the current gross annual rental, use the following formula:

$$\text{Rent multiplier} = \frac{\text{Selling price}}{\text{Gross annual rental}}$$

For example, a duplex selling for $180,000 generates $15,000 in annual rent. The rent multiplier is calculated as follows:

$$\text{Rent multiplier} = \frac{\text{Selling price}}{\text{Gross annual rental}} = \frac{\$180,000}{\$15,000} = 12$$

In other words, the property is selling for twelve times the annual rental. As I noted earlier, any property that is selling for much more than seven times the gross annual rental is probably not going to be a particularly good investment. Also remember that if you put a sizable cash down payment into the property to assure a positive cash flow, you're only fooling yourself because there's an opportunity cost associated with tying up a lot of cash that could otherwise be earning money in mutual funds, stocks, or bonds. You might be interested in knowing that professional real estate investors generally won't pay more than five to six times the gross annual rental for a property.

The Capitalization Rate Calculating the capitalization rate—or "cap rate," as the veteran real estate investors call it—is a more detailed method of evaluating a property. The cap rate is determined as follows:

$$\text{Capitalization rate} = \frac{\text{Net operating income}}{\text{Total amount invested}}$$

For example, an investor considering an investment in an apartment building requiring a total investment of $350,000 has an estimate net operating income of $30,000. The capitalization rate is calculated as follows:

$$\text{Capitalization rate} = \frac{\text{Net operating income}}{\text{Total amount invested}} = \frac{\$30,000}{\$350,000} = 8.6\%$$

A cap rate of 8 percent or higher is considered desirable.

A word to the wise: Make sure the amounts that go into the cap rate formula are realistic. The sum used for the *total amount invested* should include both the down payment and the borrowed money necessary to buy the property, while the *net operating income* is the total rental income (allowing for vacancies) less all the expenses except mortgage interest and principal repayments.

Beware of a favorite trick called "bumping to market," which is used by real estate agents and owners to make a deal look more attractive. "Bumping to market" is raising rent projections from what they actually are to what they "ought to be" according to a so-called market level. Don't believe these pie-in-the-sky projections.

Real Estate Investment Trusts

For those many of us who don't want to go through the hassle of managing our own real estate, real estate investment trusts (REITs) are an easy and inexpensive alternative. In fact, REITs were originally legislated into existence specifically to enable smaller investors to participate in the real estate market.

A REIT is a corporation that invests in real estate or mortgages. REIT shares trade on the stock exchange, so you can buy in without either the hassles of management or the problem of liquidity. As opposed to individually owned real estate parcels, REITs enjoy the advantages of diversification and professional management. Capital gains go directly to the shareholders. In addition, most REITs have paid a high dividend.

But REITs have their drawbacks as well. For one thing their

share prices get hammered in bad real estate markets just like all other real estate investments. In addition, many REITs invest in major commercial properties, which can be a problem in over-built locales. Finally, a lot of newly issued REITs have come on the market in recent years and most professionals consider them to be mediocre at best. Thus, separating the good from the not so good REIT stocks can be challenging. That's why real estate mutual funds may be the answer for wise investors who want some real estate in their investment portfolios.

Real Estate Mutual Funds

It should be pretty obvious to you what real estate mutual funds invest in. They provide an additional layer of management who helps direct your money into the most promising REIT stocks. A strong case can be made favoring real estate mutual funds over individual REIT stocks. A well-diversified real estate portfolio will include investments in several regions of the country as well as investments across several types of real estate investments like commercial, industrial, retail, and residential properties. Achieving this level of diversification with individual REIT stocks can be very costly. Indeed, it could be a full-time job. And that's what real estate mutual fund managers do for a living. They are attuned to the vagaries of real estate investing and devote themselves full time to identifying good REIT investments.

When to Sell

Deciding when to sell any investment is tough. Here are some tips regarding real estate investments.

Individually Owned Properties Timing is everything. Above all, don't sell in a weak market. If you own income-producing real estate, over the years you will inevitably have to cope with an unusually competitive market for tenants at the same time that the real estate market is weak. You must plan for the possibility that you may have to go to unusual lengths to retain and/or attract tenants, including lowering rents. Build up your cash reserves in anticipation of difficult times. Above all, you want to avoid being forced to sell your property in a weak real estate market. Ideally, you will invest in the property for the long haul. Think about the prospect of owning some income-producing real estate, eventually paying off the mortgage, and then being able to supplement your income with rents. Property can be an ideal source of *rising* retirement income.

If you have to sell or want to sell, do so when the local real estate market is hot, and expect it to take between 6 months and a year to sell the property.

REITs   Your decision to hold on to a REIT may depend on the kind of income you are receiving from it. Many may have attractive dividend yields, but such yields are hardly guaranteed. The decision on holding or selling a REIT should hinge on whether the REIT is likely to perform well over the next year. It's not unlike the decision to sell or hold a stock. In other words, if you find the REIT attractive enough to buy today, then hold on to it. If not, unload it.

REIT Mutual Funds   Once you become committed to putting a real estate mutual fund in your investment portfolio, the process of deciding to hold or sell the fund is no different from the way it is done with other mutual fund categories (see Chapter 3). Don't be surprised if your REIT mutual fund periodically underperforms all or most other funds categories. With REITs it's feast or famine, but over the long run REIT stocks and real estate mutual funds have provided average returns that are somewhat greater than the S&P 500.

The Key to Success in Buying Income-Producing Real Estate

The single most important ingredient to success is *economic viability*. If the investment relies on tax gimmicks, it could be headed for trouble. If the deal relies on capital appreciation to make any money, it's a recipe for disappointment, if not disaster. If the property relies on increasing anemic occupancy rates or raising rents, it's a pipe dream. The only worthwhile real estate investments are those that can not only survive on the basis of their own economic merits but thrive on them.

The most successful real estate investors share one characteristic—patience. If they can't get the property at the right price, they'll be quite content to sit on the sidelines. They also have the staying power to be able to survive in slow real estate markets because their properties are more than self-sustaining. I have an acquaintance who, starting from scratch, has made over $50 million in real estate, yet for the past decade, he hasn't owned any real estate. He just hasn't been able to find the right property at the right price, so he is very happy to wait until the right opportunity comes around. In the meantime, he's driving his wife crazy since he's around the house all the time.

What About Undeveloped Land?

You may think that undeveloped land could be an ideal first-time real estate investment, but it is often the worst. Why? Raw land purchases often end up being raw deals. Successful investors in undeveloped land need deep pockets—and more. Since undeveloped land doesn't generate any income, your money will be tied up for a long time. It's difficult to finance undeveloped land for more than a few years. In addition, finding the right kind of property takes some real expertise. Another cautionary note: Large parcels of land that sell for peanuts usually spell trouble, not bargain. The price is cheap for a number of good reasons—lousy location, difficult access, bad drainage. So if the land you want to purchase has more moose per square mile than people, don't expect to make any money on it. Land in particularly desirable areas, on the other hand, is always very expensive to purchase.

CHAPTER 15

———— ∞∞∞ ————

Investing for Kids

Kids and money—Yikes!!! While I've often said, "Never take financial responsibility for anything that eats," I don't always practice what I preach. Truth be told, I've got three daughters and like all parents my wife and I struggle to:

1. Figure out a way to invest college savings so that they can grow enough to help pay those gargantuan college costs, and
2. Teach the kids about money and investing. My objective here is to help our munchkins become financially responsible so my wife and I won't have to support *them* in our old age, if that's possible anymore.

In this chapter, I'll share some of my ideas on both. So if you're a parent—or a grandparent—this chapter's for you.

Investing for College

I get very depressed when I look at the projections of how much it's going to cost to educate my kids. As near as I can figure, it costs roughly the equivalent of two houses to educate one child. When I add it up for three kids, college bills look more like the federal budget deficit than a college cost projection. By the way, don't even think about trying to save every last cent it's going to cost to educate Junior. It will require your putting aside more money than you could possibly afford. Instead, plan on setting aside each month an amount that you can reasonably afford— perhaps enough to cover 30 to 40 percent of the cost. According to some of my lucky friends whose kids have finished college, just having the kids out of the house during college will save enough on living expenses to make up the difference!

What a Difference a Few Percentage Points Make

Of course, saving for college on a regular basis is essential to meeting college costs without putting either you or your child into big-time hock. But investing those college savings so that they'll grow is also key—and it's an area where a lot of parents fall down. The following sidebar shows how much difference *investing*, rather than just saving, college-bound money can make by the time the tuition bills come rolling in. Both the Savers' family and the Investors' family save the same amount of money—$300 each month for fifteen years, right up until their young scholars enter the ivy-covered halls of learning. How much do they accumulate? Well, it depends on how the money is invested. The Savers put the money in safe, but low-yield savings and short-term CDS that pay only 4 percent interest. Far too many parents invest college money that conservatively—if you can call that investing at all. It's really saving, not investing. The Investor family, on the other hand, took some risk with the money so that it had a chance to grow. They average 8 percent a year over the first ten years that they invest the money, and then, as their youngster nears college age, they begin to invest that money more conserva-tively (more on that later). So the annual return over the last five years drops to 5 percent. It doesn't take an MIT or Cal

Tech mathematician to see from the information below that investing the money—as opposed to just hiding it in a savings account—makes a lot of difference.

The Difference Between Saving and Investing College Money

Sarah and Sam Savers

This family saves $300 per month for fifteen years, earning 4 percent annual interest. At the end of fifteen years, the college fund has $74,000.

Ivan and Irene Investors

This family invests $300 per month for fifteen years, earning an 8 percent return over the first ten years and a 5 percent return over the last five years. At the end of fifteen years, the college fund is worth $91,000—$17,000 more than the Savers!

How to Invest College Money

How you invest money that's earmarked for college depends a lot on how long it is before you'll need to use the money. And that, of course, depends on your child's age. The nearer the child is to entering college, the less risk you can afford with the money that will be needed to meet college costs.

There aren't many times in our lives when we are investing for the short term, but one of those times is when a child nears college age. Here are my suggestions:

Preteens If the child is under thirteen, invest the money just as you would any long-term money, as I described in Chapters 1 and 2. The majority of the money—certainly at least 60 percent will be invested in stock mutual funds and perhaps individual stocks.

Teenagers As if having a teenager isn't worrisome enough already, you're also going to need to spend some time worrying about his or her college funds. The trick here is to gradually shift your money out of stocks into more conservative investments. Why? Because you're becoming short-term investors, since college is now just a few years off. Therefore, if you're definitely going to need the money for tuition, you don't want to risk having too much money invested in stocks that could, of course, take a tumble just before the tuition bills come due.

Table 15-1 is a timetable that shows one way to change the way college investments are allocated gradually.

Table 15-1

Timetable for Gradually Changing Investment Allocation as College Age Approaches

AGE	12	13	14	15	16	17	18
Stock Funds	60%	50%	40%	30%	20%	10%	10%
Long-Term Bond Funds	30%	30%	30%	20%	10%	–	–
Short-Term Bond Funds	10%	10%	10%	20%	30%	40%	30%
Cash	–	10%	20%	30%	40%	50%	60%
	100%	100%	100%	100%	100%	100%	100%

Some Other Matters to Consider

In addition to these general guidelines, there are some other important college savings matters to consider.

The Family Wealth Factor   Moving to a more conservative investment allocation as the child nears college age is particularly important if you have limited resources outside of the college nest egg to draw upon. If, on the other hand, you're fortunate enough to have enough money to be able to pay the tuition bills from other sources, then you may not need to become as conservative with the college funds as I outlined above. In other words, you have enough backup money to be able to continue taking some risk with the college fund.

Custodial Account?   Should you keep the college savings fund in your name or your child's name? There certainly are tax advantages for putting at least *some* money in the youngster's name. A limited amount of investment income earned in a custodial account for a child under age fourteen is taxed at the child's lower tax rate; for the fourteen-and-over set, there are no such "kiddie tax" limitations.

But putting too much money in a child's name can backfire. First, there is no absolute guarantee that your darling will spend the money on a Princeton education. Once children reach the age of majority (age eighteen in most states), they can't legally be stopped from using the money any way they want. Imagine this scenario: In lieu of going to college, your daughter joins a cult and falls in love with the chief guru. His highness urges her to "release" herself from all worldly goods (so that he can buy another Rolls-Royce with your money, of course). This has happened!

Second, building up a cache of money in your child's name could be a liability if you think you may qualify for financial aid. Why? Because under the complex formula for calculating how much aid a student is eligible for, the expected contribution from investments in a child's name is much higher than the expected contribution had those investments remained in the parent's name.

So what's the upshot here? My advice is to put some money in a young child's name—to take advantage of the lower taxes. Once the child reaches the teen years, and you can be at least somewhat more certain about his responsibility and college aspirations, shift more money to the child if you're pretty sure you won't qualify for college financial aid.

State Tuition Savings Plans   Many states now offer tuition savings plans. Are these a worthwhile place to invest college money? As with most matters financial, it depends. The money you contribute to these plans is put into municipal bonds, so the main attraction is tax-exempt interest. Some of the programs are quite attractive, others are not as attractive. In general, the investment returns are best if the child goes to one of the participating colleges—usually a state college. But if the child opts for another college—most parents would prefer not to restrict their kid's college choice—then the returns will be much lower. If you are attracted to your state's tuition savings plan, go ahead and participate, but with only some of your college savings—25 percent, perhaps. Consider this money to be a rock-solid foundation for your college savings. But don't go overboard here, because you can probably get higher investment returns elsewhere.

The Family House as a Source of Tuition Payments   I'm not talking here about taking out a home equity loan to help pay college costs, but this may become necessary. Instead, some families try to pay off the home mortgage by the time their kids go off to get their higher learning. No mortgage means more money each month that can be used to pay college costs. Not a bad idea, if you can afford to pay off the mortgage that soon.

Investments to Avoid

Although you may be told differently, there are a couple of investments that don't make much sense for college savings. Don't get me wrong, these are certainly better than nothing, but you can probably do better. Cash value life insurance, insuring either you, your spouse, or worse, your child, won't deliver the kinds of returns you need to build up a sizable college nest egg. U.S. savings bonds were once an okay investment, but when they changed the rules in 1995, they pretty much spoiled them. One exception to this is if you can reasonably expect to use the savings bonds to pay tuition costs and your income at the time college rolls around falls under certain limitations. If so, the accumulated savings bond interest will be tax-free. Even then, however, your return won't be all that great.

Teaching Kids About Investing

There is a crisis in family values in this country. In the old days, parents used to be able to rely on their children to support them in their old age. But, alas, today it's not just that our children won't support us anymore, it's the parents in their golden years who are supporting their children. This is most certainly a crisis! The way I figure it, the more we as parents can do to teach our children about money and investing, the more likely the kids are to leave the family dole eventually. Here are some ideas on how you can use investments to provide children and grandchildren with a gift that will pay lifelong dividends—the gift of financial literacy.

Youngsters

The best way to introduce young children to investing is either to give them some money to invest or require them to set aside a portion of their allowances for investing. If it's a small amount of money, the only choice may be to "invest" the money in a savings account. But even then, a youngster can learn that money that is put away (rather than spent) can grow. This is an important lesson. Later on, the child might be encouraged to invest some money in a mutual fund or stock. She might not show any interest at first, but at least you have provided her with the opportunity to learn about investing later on. My grandmother introduced me to investing when I was eleven with a gift of a few shares of General Motors and Chase Manhattan Bank. I didn't know what they were at first, but I still remember the excitement of looking up their prices in the newspaper. Incidentally, gifts of stock or mutual fund investments are more educational than no-risk savings accounts or saving bonds because with stocks and mutual funds kids learn one of the most important rules of successful investing: the best investments will periodically decline in value.

High School and College

Most teenagers will sooner or later begin to show an interest in investing. Continue encouraging them by giving them some money to invest, if you can afford it. Their stock choices may seem narrow to you (teens seem to opt for stocks of companies that produce fast food or athletic shoes), but don't discourage them.

Here's a dynamite idea: Set up an IRA for a kid. As long as the child earns income outside the home (allowances or money earned around the house don't count), he can set up and contribute to an IRA—or you can give him the money to put into an IRA. Mowing lawns, babysitting, after-school jobs, and summer jobs all qualify. Think of the valuable lessons you impart to a child who has an IRA: tax shelter, because the IRA is probably deductible; the power of tax-deferred growth, the importance of saving for retirement even when it's forty or fifty years away. By the way, most mutual fund companies will allow IRAs to be set up for minors. If you start young enough, the power of compound growth is staggering. Just look at Table 15-2 to see how much a single $1,000 IRA contribution will amass by the time the early saver reaches retirement age.

Table 15-2

How Much a Single IRA Contribution Will Grow—If You Start Early

AGE	ONE-TIME IRA CONTRIBUTION	VALUE AT AGE 65 AT 9% ANNUAL GROWTH
20	$1,000	$48,000
17	1,000	62,000
14	1,000	81,000

Young Adults Your high school or college graduate finally got a job. Hallelujah! Now, if you can spare the money, here's a way to leave a legacy to your children or grandchildren that will last a lifetime. Think back when you got your first real job. Expenses were high—rent, furniture, clothes, car payments. It's no different today. Just making ends meet is tough enough. Saving some money? Forget it.

Here's where parents or grandparents can come to the rescue. Give the new careerist a cash gift with the proviso that the money will either go into her employer's retirement savings plan or into an IRA. Either way, you can show the young adult how important *you* think it is that they start putting away money for retirement. That attitude will be contagious.

One Last Thought

Whether your child or grandchild is five, fifteen, or twenty-five, one of the best ways to teach her about money is to discuss family investments in her presence. You don't have to have a huge portfolio to do this. But show her that investing is a part of everyday life—and an important part at that. Several years ago I conducted a study on the background and upbringing of leading investment managers. These pros came from a myriad of educational, career, and economic backgrounds, but the majority of them had one thing in common: They first learned about investing from their parents.

CHAPTER 16

———∞∞∞———

What to Do If You Have
a Lot of Cash to Invest

There may come a time (or that time could be right now) when you have a lot of money sitting in a checking or savings account or other low-yield securities that you want to invest. There are a couple of events that could give rise to this:

1. Up to this point, you haven't done anything about investing all or a large chunk of the money you have saved.
2. You have recently received a cash windfall, perhaps an inheritance or a distribution from your retirement plan or a large bonus (lucky you). Whatever the situation, the $64,000 question is, *How fast should you go about investing the money?*

There are two schools of thought about how to invest a sizable amount of cash. The first school says: "Invest it all at once." And it has history on its side. More often than not, the stock market is rising—in fact it rises about 80 percent of the time. Therefore, you've got the odds in your favor, so invest all the money at once. Historical studies that have compared immediate investing with gradual investing do show that there is a slight advantage in investing all the money at once.

Now for the second school of thought. Let's call it "Jonathan's Sleep-at-Night Approach." I prefer investing a cash windfall gradually, because I couldn't sleep at night investing a lot of money all at once. (Of course, if the market recently took a big tumble, and/or interest rates were sky high, I might be more inclined to invest the money all at once.) I'm not alone in this theory, by the way. A lot of investment pros think that history be damned, you don't want to risk making a major investment in stocks just before the market declines or a major investment in bonds just before interest rates shoot up.

Moreover, investors with a lot of cash to invest may become so wary of a possible loss that they end up doing nothing with the money other than letting it languish in low-interest investments. The way to reduce the risk of ill-timed investing is to devise a plan to invest your money gradually. Don't get me wrong. If you can accept the risk of investing all of the money at once, then do it. History is on your side. But a lot of us are a bit too skittish to do that.

IT'S LIKE DOLLAR-COST AVERAGING. Investing your money gradually is, in essence, much like the dollar-cost averaging technique that is widely and successfully used for investing in individual stocks or mutual funds. In fact, if you are participating in a retirement savings plan at work or are contributing to an IRA every year or are otherwise investing money on a regular basis, you are already dollar-cost averaging into the stock and bond markets.

Setting Up an Investment Timetable

If you are more comfortable gradually investing your cash, you need to set up an investment timetable. This will allow you to take a disciplined approach to investing the money, so that

you won't be swayed by changing market conditions. If you
don't follow the timetable because you're concerned about
market conditions, you risk keeping the money in cash too
long. Table 16-1 shows a typical investment timetable over a
period of eighteen months. Note that the allocations in the
column entitled "18 months hence" are the target allocations
that were established in Steps One and Two of my four easy
steps to successful investing. You'll find them in Chapters 1
and 2. In this example, and it is only an illustration of how
this is done, the target investment allocation is 70 percent
stocks and 30 percent bonds. As the timetable also indicates,
while 20 percent of the money is invested in stocks and stock
funds immediately and 15 percent invested in long-term bond
funds immediately, the majority of the cash initially sits on
the sidelines in either money market funds or short-term
bond funds.

Within the first 12 months of the investment program, stock
exposure is increased from 20 to 50 percent. And finally, eighteen months hence, this illustration reflects the investor's target allocation. You may want to devise your gradual investment
program over a shorter or longer period. The important thing
is to follow your timetable once it is set up. Of course, if
during the interim there is a major change in the investment
markets, such as a major decline in stock prices or a sharp rise
in interest rates, you may want to accelerate your investment
program somewhat to take advantage of more favorable investment conditions.

Gradually investing a lot of cash or a financial windfall often
makes a lot of sense, particularly when you think stock prices
are unusually high and/or interest rates are temporarily low.
Certainly, opportunities may be missed by following such a
timetable, but on the other hand, costly mistakes may also
be avoided.

Table 16-1

Taking Your Time to Invest

SAMPLE TIMETABLE FOR INVESTING CASH OR A
FINANCIAL WINDFALL

PERCENTAGE ALLOCATION

	Now	6 months hence	12 months hence	18 months hence
STOCK AND STOCK MUTUAL FUNDS				
Growth	5	5	10	15
Growth and Income	5	10	15	20
Small company	5	10	10	15
International	5	10	15	20
Subtotal stock and stock mutual funds	20	35	50	70
BOND AND BOND MUTUAL FUNDS				
Corporate: •Short/intermediate	10	5	5	–
•Long-term	5	5	5	5
U.S. Government: •Short/Intermediate	10	10	5	5
•Long-term	5	5	5	5
Municipal: •Short/intermediate	10	5	5	5
•Long-term	5	10	10	10
Subtotal bonds and bond funds	45	40	35	30
MONEY MARKET FUNDS	35	25	15	–
Total	100	100	100	100

CHAPTER 17

How to Invest Money That
You're Going to Need
Within a Few Years

The four easy steps to investment success apply to money
that you can afford to put away indefinitely. But all of
us also need to put aside money for short-term needs, if
for no other reason than to have a little bit set aside for
financial emergencies. Also, any time you can be certain
that you'll need the money within a few years, you will need
to invest that money more conservatively. Here are some
examples of situations where you will need to invest
conservatively:

- A small emergency fund
- Saving for a house
- Saving for a car
- Saving for home improvements
- Saving for college tuition when college is just a few
  years away

There are many short-term investment alternatives, so you need not necessarily confine your short-term savings to low- or no-yield accounts. In fact, by carefully comparing the yields offered by various short-term investment securities, you can make the most of your money. After all, why settle for a 3 percent return in a savings account when you may be able to get almost twice that in other safe, short-term investments? In fact, you can change from one to another quickly and without concern about capital-gains taxes or fees. Since short-term investments maintain a stable principal value you generally incur no capital gain or loss when you sell it. In some rare instances, primarily with Treasury bills, you may have a small capital gain or loss. Concerning fees, you can generally move from one short-term investment to another without paying a fee. Two exceptions: You generally pay a small fee to sell and buy a Treasury bill. Also, if you sell a CD before maturity, you will get hit with a penalty—usually either one month's worth of interest or six month's worth of interest, depending upon the CD's maturity. But all in all, taxes and fees are almost always of little concern when it comes to buying and selling short-term investments.

Finding the Best Returns on Short-Term Investments

As opposed to stocks and bonds, short-term investments are pretty straightforward, if not bland. But with a little bit of effort, you can make the most of these otherwise mundane investments. The keys to success are as follows:

1. Determining the current interest rates paid by various kinds of short-term investments
2. Comparing after-tax interest rates to find the investment with the best return

The first step is pretty easy. The financial pages of most newspapers regularly show the interest being paid on most types of short-term investments. If you really want to do a bang-up job, buy a copy of *Barron's* at the newsstand. It has extensive and up-to-date data on the interest paid on all types of short-term investments.

Once you've determined the interest that is being paid on the various short-term investments, the next step is to determine which pays the most. This is easier said than done, however, because the way short-term investments are taxed varies.

So if a money market deposit account at the bank pays 4.1 percent interest, but your mutual fund company offers a tax-exempt money market fund that pays 3.6 percent, it may seem that the bank money market deposit account is better. But the interest income on a tax-exempt money market fund is not subject to federal income tax, while the money market deposit account is. Therefore, even though the stated interest rate on a particular short-term investment may be lower, it's how much you get to keep after taxes that counts.

The following tables will help you make the most of your short-term investments by finding which pay the highest interest after taxes have been taken out. (They can also be helpful in figuring out the best deals on various types of bonds and bond funds.)

Table 17-1 shows how the various short-term investments are taxed.

Table 17-2 is a summary worksheet that you can use to compare interest rates on short-term investments that you are considering.

Tables 17-3, 17-4, and 17-5 provide worksheets that will enable you to calculate comparable interest rates for investments whose interest is exempt from federal and/or state income taxes. Once you determine the comparable interest rates on any or all of these tables, you should transfer these amounts to Table 17-2. Finally, **Table 17-6** provides a shortcut to help you complete Table 17-5.

These tables may seem a bit intimidating. But they aren't difficult to fill out, and your time and effort will be well rewarded.

Table 17-1

Summary of How Short-Term Investments Are Taxed

TYPE OF SHORT-TERM INVESTMENT	INTEREST INCOME IS SUBJECT TO:	
	Federal income taxes	State income taxes
AVAILABLE THROUGH BANKS:		
Savings accounts	Yes	Yes
Money market deposit accounts	Yes	Yes
AVAILABLE THROUGH MUTUAL FUNDS OR BROKERS:		
General money market funds	Yes	Yes
U.S. Treasury money market funds	Yes	No
Tax-exempt money market funds	No	Yes
Single-state tax-exempt money market funds	No	No
AVAILABLE THROUGH BANKS OR BROKERS:		
U.S. Treasury bills	Yes	No
Short-term CDs	Yes	Yes

Table 17-2

It's How Much You Get to Keep After Taxes That Counts

WORKSHEET TO COMPARE INTEREST PAID ON SHORT-TERM INVESTMENTS

Type of short-term investment	Current interest rate	Comparable interest rate
AVAILABLE THROUGH BANKS:		
Savings accounts	___%	___%[1]
Money market deposit accounts	___%	___%[1]

Type of short-term investment	Current interest rate	Comparable interest rate
AVAILABLE THROUGH MUTUAL FUNDS OR BROKERS:		
General money market funds	___%	___%[1]
U.S. Treasury money market funds	___%	___%[2]
Tax-exempt money market funds	___%	___%[3]
Single-state tax-exempt money market funds	___%	___%[4]
AVAILABLE THROUGH BANKS OR BROKERS:		
Treasury bills	___%	___%[2]
Short-term CDs	___%	___%[1]

[1] Comparable interest rate is the same as the current interest rate since the interest is subject to both federal and state income taxes.

[2] Use Table 17-3 to calculate the comparable interest rate.

[3] Use Table 17-4 to calculate the comparable interest rate.

[4] Use Table 17-5 to calculate the comparable interest rate.

——————— Table 17-3 ———————

Worksheet to Determine the Comparable Interest Rate for an Investment That Is Subject to State Income Taxes but Is Exempt from Federal Income Taxes

		Example
1. Interest rate on investment	___%	3.1%
2. Your federal income tax rate converted to a decimal (for example 28% = .28)	___	.28
3. Amount in step 2 subtracted from 1.00	___	.72
4. Comparable interest rate: The amount in step 1 divided by the amount in step 3	___	4.3

Note: This worksheet should be used for tax-exempt money market funds that invest in several states. (Use Table 17-5 for single-state tax exempt money market funds.)

EXAMPLE: Allison Anderson wants to know how much a tax-exempt money market fund that currently yields 3.1 percent would compare with a fully taxable money market fund paying 4 percent interest. Allison is in the 28 percent tax bracket. By using the above worksheet (Table 17–3), she finds that the comparable yield for the tax-exempt money market fund is 4.3 percent. So, while it has a lower yield than the taxable money market fund, after taxes have been factored in, she is better off with the tax-exempt money market fund.

Table 17-4

Worksheet to Determine the Comparable Interest Rate for an Investment That Is Subject to Federal Income Taxes but Is Exempt from State Income Taxes

		Example
1. Interest rate on investment	__%	4.7%
2. Your state income tax rate on interest income converted to a decimal (for example 4% = .04)	__	.04
3. Amount in step 1 subtracted from 1.00	__	.96
4. Comparable interest rate: The amount in step 1 divided by the amount in step 3	__%	4.9%

Note: This worksheet should be used for U.S. Treasury bills or money market funds that invest exclusively in U.S. Treasury bills

---

EXAMPLE: Barney Billingsgate wants to park his money for a year in either a 5.25 percent CD or in a U.S. Treasury bill that pays 4.7 percent. While the T-bill pays lower interest, the interest on it is not subject to state income tax. Barney wonders whether this will actually make the

T-bill a better investment than the CD. He works out the numbers using Table 17-4, factoring in his 4 percent state income tax rate on interest income, and finds that the comparable yield on the T-bill is 4.9 percent, or considerably lower than the CD interest rate. He wisely opts for the CD.

Table 17-5

Worksheet to Determine Comparable Interest Rate for an Investment That Is Exempt from Both Federal and State Income Taxes

		Example
1. Your federal income tax bracket	___%	28 %
2. Your state income tax on interest income	___	5
3. State tax-free equivalent multiplier (based on your federal income tax bracket and state income tax rate) The multiplier can be found in Table 17-6.		1.46
4. Interest rate paid on investment whose interest is exempt from both federal and state taxes	×___	× 3.1
5. Interest rate in step 4 multiplied by the multiplier in step 3 equals the comparable yield on a fully taxable investment	___%	4.5 %

Note: This worksheet should be used for single-state tax-exempt money market funds if you are a resident of that state. (Use Table 17-3 for tax-exempt money market funds that invest in several states.)

─────────────── **Table 17-6** ───────────────

Multiplier Based on Your Federal and State Income Tax Brackets

YOUR STATE TAX RATE ON INTEREST INCOME	YOUR FEDERAL INCOME TAX BRACKET				
	15%	28%	31%	36%	39.6%
2	1.20	1.42	1.48	1.59	1.69
3	1.21	1.43	1.49	1.61	1.71
4	1.23	1.45	1.51	1.63	1.72
5	1.24	1.46	1.53	1.64	1.74
6	1.25	1.48	1.54	1.66	1.76
7	1.27	1.49	1.56	1.68	1.78
8	1.28	1.51	1.58	1.70	1.80
9	1.29	1.53	1.59	1.72	1.82
10	1.31	1.54	1.61	1.74	1.84
11	1.32	1.56	1.68	1.76	1.86
12	1.34	1.58	1.70	1.78	1.88

Note: The multipliers apply only to interest, not total return (i.e., interest plus capital gains).

EXAMPLE: Carolyn Carroll thinks her friend has lost her mind. They both have investments at the same mutual fund company, and her friend said that the mutual fund company's single-state tax-exempt money market fund, which yields just 3.1 percent, is actually a better deal than the taxable money market fund in which Carolyn has her emergency money and that pays 4.25 percent. Well, Carolyn worked out the specifics as described in Table 17-5 and found, to her dismay, the paltry 3.1 percent yield on the single-state money market fund was actually better, after taxes had been factored in, than the much larger 4.25 percent interest on the fully taxable money market fund.

Some Final Tips

Here are a few final suggestions to help you make the most of your short-term investments.

CD Shopping

If you are in the market for a CD, a little shopping around—even outside your hometown, could reap some rewards. First, however, compare rates among banks in town. CDs are a competitive business these days. If you have a broker check with him or her about CD offerings that the brokerage firm may have. Finally, if you are in the market for a high-yielding CD, *Barron's* lists the highest yielding CDs in the country each week. Remember, as long as the issuing bank is FDIC insured, your really shouldn't care where your CD comes from. You just want the best yield.

Compare Money Market Fund Yields

If you have an account with a mutual fund or broker that offers several different kinds of money market funds, be sure to compare yields, as I explained earlier in this chapter, to make sure you're getting the best after-tax return. This may require you to compare the returns periodically among various money market funds, but hey, if you can improve your return by periodically switching among money market funds, it's more money in your pocket.

Save on Treasury Bill Purchases

If you regularly buy T-bills, consider buying them directly from the U.S. Treasury at no cost. Simply call the nearest Federal Reserve bank or branch and ask for some information on their "Treasury Direct" program. If you don't want to go through the effort of buying T-bills directly from the Fed, compare fees between your bank and your brokerage firm.

CHAPTER 18

---∞---

The Most Important Financial Decision of Your Life: How to Handle a Retirement Plan Distribution When You Retire

There are several watershed moments in most of our lives. Our graduation, our wedding day, the birth of a child are all days that we will never forget. (Isn't it interesting that each of these moments leaves us impoverished—at least temporarily.) But for many of us, the most important financial decision of our lives is still before us—how to handle a distribution from our retirement plan when we are ready to retire.

Is it better to take a lump-sum payout at retirement, or to take an annuity? The answer to that is anything but simple, the ramifications can be huge, and it is made even more perplexing by the general lack of objective advice on the subject. Investment advisers will likely encourage us to roll our benefits over into an IRA, while those in the annuity business will quote chapter and verse on the virtues of annuitizing.

True, some pension plans make it easy: They don't give you

a choice—you are required to take an annuity when you retire, period. On the other hand, many plans allow you the option of taking a lump-sum payment, which affords you the considerable advantage of giving you much more control over your financial destiny, now that you know how to invest wisely and well. Of course, this option must be considered very carefully.

Important Considerations

As I mentioned, you may not be able to find an unbiased opinion, but that's why I'm here—to give you the straight scoop. Here are the matters to consider.

Investment Risk

Once you take possession of your lump sum, what happens to it is your business. If you lose it in unwise investments or even "wise" ones that go sour anyway—there is no recourse but to suffer in silence. If you don't have a high degree of confidence in your own investment abilities—or those of a qualified investment adviser—you may be better off taking an annuity with all or a sizable portion of your pension distribution.

Liability Risk

Lump-sum distributions may be subject to attachment if you exhaust other resources with major medical (or other) expenses, including nursing home costs in the years ahead. In many cases, though, annuities are not subject to attachment.

Inflation Risk

While some annuity plans are adjusted (at least partly) to offset the effects of inflation, most are not. The reality of a fixed-payout annuity is a steady loss of purchasing power. At 3½ percent annual inflation, your annuity will lose one-half of its purchasing power in twenty years. On the other hand, if you take the lump sum, you have a good, but by no means assured, chance of investing it so that it allows you to keep up with inflation.

Expected Income

In general, annuity payouts give you less income than you could make if you were investing the money on your own. Reason: The annuity payout schedules tend to be figured very conservatively to minimize the insurance company's future financial risk. Be sure to find out the exact monthly payment you'd receive from an annuity and compare this figure to your anticipated rate of return if you were investing a lump sum on your own.

Mortality Risk

Traditionally, annuity payments cease when you do. Consequently, if you die prematurely, your estate is considerably poorer than it would have been if you'd taken a lump sum.

Note, though, that many annuity plans—both the corporate type and kind you buy on your own—make some sort of provision for this event. Typically it's a continuation of some lesser stream of payments for the benefit of a surviving spouse, or the option of receiving a lump-sum payout of the undistributed portion of the principal underlying the annuity. Often, you can select from a menu of payout options.

The Annuity Option

While there are as many different varieties of annuities as there are butterflies in the Amazon, the basic setup is quite straightforward. The annuity issuer determines the amount of payments based on two factors: current interest rates and your current life expectancy. The payment combines both interest earned on the lump sum and a rebate of your principal over time, with the idea that all your principal will have been returned to you (with interest) by the time you reach your life expectancy (which is a polite way of saying at the time the insurance company bets you're going to die). Note that just because the annuity issuer has returned your entire investment doesn't mean the payments will stop. They keep on chugging along as long as you do. Clearly then, the way to "beat the system" with an annuity is to outlive the mortality table's prediction of your life expectancy.

Note too that while an annuity's monthly payment may look pretty impressive—perhaps 10 percent of your principal on an annual basis—this represents not a return on your money but at least partly a return of your money. And the part of the payment that's a return on your money—the interest earned—can look pretty paltry. Why? Because the insurance company has to make a provision for interest rates declining, which could lower the return they would make on your money, together with the chance that you'll outlive Methuselah.

The Lump-Sum Rollover Option

Rolling a pension distribution over into an IRA certainly provides more flexibility than taking an annuity, from which there is no turning back. (Some individuals born on or before December 31, 1935, may have another option called "averaging" a lump-sum distribution. You'll need to check with a Certified Public Accountant to see if averaging makes sense.) In a nutshell, a lump sum gives you the opportunity not only to derive income to meet retirement living expenses, but also to preserve, if not grow, your capital. But you should be comfortable with the risks that come with investing for both growth and income. Investing your lump sum for both growth and income shouldn't make you overly concerned, however. The important thing to remember is that your distribution won't grow in an annuity, and, of course, you will never make any (or enough) headway if you roll the distribution over into a money market fund, CD, or other safe, but low-yielding investment.

Don't Procrastinate

For heaven's sake don't wait until the last minute to decide what you want to do with a pension distribution. It's too important to leave until the last minute. Whatever you decide to do, remember to instruct your employer to send the distribution directly to the institution that will hold the money or to the plan of your new employer (a so-called trustee-to-trustee rollover). If you receive the money yourself, (1) your employer is required to withhold 20 percent of the distribution, and (2) you must complete the rollover within 60 days or the entire distribution will be subject to tax. Ugh!

Okay, What Should You Do?

Lump-sum rollover or annuity? Each payout method has its advantages and disadvantages. Here are my thoughts on this crucial decision:

• **No financial decision is either/or.** Many retirees will benefit from taking an annuity for part of the money and investing the rest.

• **If you do decide on an annuity, be sure to shop around.** Don't assume that the annuity your company offers or the first annuity your insurance agent offers is the best. It may not be. The annuity business is very competitive, so it pays to compare. But don't necessarily take the highest offer it if comes from a mediocre insurance company. Be sure to annuitize only with an insurance company that's in top-notch financial shape.

• **If you decide to accept a lump-sum payment, make sure you examine the best way to put more of your retirement dollars in your pocket and less in Uncle Sam's.** That usually means continuing to defer taking any money out of the IRA, even if you have to tap into investments in your taxable accounts. (See Chapter 11.)

• **If you are receiving a lump-sum distribution *before* retirement, your choice is usually between rolling it over into an IRA or into the new employer's plan.** Of course, you could also take the money out and spend it, but I'm not even going to comment on how incredibly shortsighted that is. After all, this is a family publication. Anyway, the best choice is to roll it over into an IRA, because with an IRA you have virtually unlimited investment options. Chances are your new employer's plan will have more limited investment choices.

• **Here's one final thought that works very well for many new retirees.** Consider rolling over the entire amount of the distribution into an IRA and then eventually using some of it to purchase an annuity. For example, you may want to wait until you are in your seventies to purchase an annuity. By postponing the annuity purchase, you can increase the amount of income that the annuity will pay out since the payments are tied to life expectancy. So long as you are comfortable investing all of the distribution, there may be no need to rush into an annuity at the time you retire.

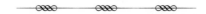

Buyer Beware: Pension Maximization Insurance

Be aware and wary of this retirement-funding technique that has been promoted by the insurance industry and many employers: Opting for a single life annuity (rather than a joint life annuity with your spouse) and buying a life insurance policy to provide for your spouse. As you probably know, single life annuities provide payments only during *your* life—they do not continue payments to your spouse upon your death. (A joint-and-survivor annuity does provide payments to your surviving spouse.) What's the attraction of a single life annuity? Higher monthly payments. That's why some companies (often in their zeal to encourage employees to retire early) have been endorsing the use of pension maximization insurance.

Theoretically, part of those larger pension payments could be used to buy an insurance policy on your life, in order to provide insurance proceeds for your spouse in lieu of a continuing annuity. This is what the insurance industry is touting, and it can work in many instances. But there are potential problems. Can you afford sufficient life insurance coverage? Cash value insurance gets pretty expensive for people nearing retirement age. Can you keep up the payments? What happens if the insurance company gets into financial trouble? In addition, your spouse must be capable of managing the life insurance proceeds effectively in order to ensure a continuing income after you're gone. This may be particularly difficult if your spouse is unacquainted with managing money, elderly, or in poor health. Thus, any strategy that uses life insurance in lieu of a joint annuity must be evaluated over and over again. It may sound like a good idea and it may be, but often it isn't.

CHAPTER 19

Investing When You're Retired

There's a popular myth that once you're retired, you've got to make some major changes in the way you invest. Wrong! As you'll see in this chapter, while retirees usually have to confront some major financial decisions, making big changes in the way you invest is not one of them—assuming you have invested wisely during your working years.

Time to Take Charge of Your Investments

When you retire, you will be delighted to find that, perhaps for the first time in your life, you have the time available to devote to your investing. And all I can say is, "Go for it." With experience and time on your side, you'll become a much better investor—whether you make all your investment decisions yourself or rely on someone else to guide you. I am acquainted with one woman who had never done any investing until just after she retired. She decided that it was high time she learned about investing, so she joined an investment club.

To make a long story short, in twenty years she has turned $100,000 into well over $1 million. And she is still a very successful, active investor in her mid-eighties.

Retirees Need to Invest for Both Growth and Income

Whenever I hear retirees on one of the radio talk shows go over their portfolios—consisting of CDs, savings accounts, and bonds—I cringe. Why? Because while most retirees certainly need income from their investments to help meet living expenses, they also need growth. Take a gander at Table 19-1, which shows just how much living costs can increase over a (hopefully) long retirement. It shows how much living expenses increase at a 3½ percent average annual rate of inflation. How, pray tell, could anyone be able to keep up with inflation if his or her portfolio doesn't grow?

―――――――――――――――― **Table 19-1** ――――――――――――――――

Why Investing for Growth Is Important for Retirees

AGE	LIVING EXPENSES ADJUSTED FOR 3½% AVERAGE ANNUAL INFLATION					
65	$20,000	$30,000	$40,000	$50,000	$60,000	$70,000
70	24,000	36,000	48,000	59,000	72,000	71,000
75	28,000	42,000	56,000	71,000	85,000	99,000
80	34,000	50,000	67,000	84,000	100,000	117,000
85	40,000	60,000	80,000	99,000	119,000	139,000
90	47,000	71,000	94,000	118,000	142,000	165,000
95	56,000	84,000	112,000	140,000	168,000	196,000
100	67,000	100,000	133,000	167,000	200,000	233,000

EXAMPLE: Ralph Retiree, age sixty-five, is getting ready to
retire, and he estimates that his living expenses in his first
year of retirement will be $30,000. Ralph is a little surprised
to see how much his cost of living will increase at a 3½
percent rate of inflation (and inflation could be higher than
that). By age seventy-five, his cost of living has gone up by
more than 50 percent. It will cost him $42,000 to live on
what had cost him $30,000 just a decade earlier. And it gets
worse. By age eighty-five his cost of living will have doubled,
and if he makes it to age 100 (and more and more seniors
are) his cost of living will have more than tripled to
$100,000!

So how should a retiree invest? Is there anything that should
be done to your investments when you retire? The best way
to look at this is to examine the following case study.

CASE STUDY:
Fine Tuning a Retirement Portfolio

Background

Andy and Sue Owings are just about to retire, and they're
hearing a lot of conflicting information about how they
should invest their retirement money. "We're in a real
quandary," notes Sue. "We'll be retiring in about six
months. Of course, we're concerned about what changes
we should make to our investments. But the advice we
are hearing or reading about is all over the place."

Andy adds, "Let me give you an idea of how divergent
the opinions are. At one extreme is my eighty-eight-year-
old father who says that it's crucial to keep retirement
money safe. To this day, his idea of a good retirement
investment is a CD or Treasury bill. At the other extreme

is an article I read recently that suggested that new retirees should actually become more aggressive in the way they invest, because of the need for investments to grow during retirement to keep up with rising living costs. I think we've been pretty aggressive over the years already, and the notion of taking even more risk is not very comforting at this point.

"In between these two extremes, Sue and I have had friends who tell us that bonds are the place to be because retirees need income and can't afford the risk of a bear stock market. Another acquaintance said that if we're happy with the way we are investing now, there is really no reason to change the way we invest just because we're retired. You know, the problem Sue and I are having is that all of these suggestions, even the extreme ones, have an element of good sense in them. This makes it even tougher to decide what we should do. I guess our biggest concern is that we don't want to make a major mistake. After all, we are no longer in our twenties and thirties where we would have plenty of time to make up for a bad investment or bad investment strategy. We don't have enough money to be able to afford that luxury at this point."

Investment Objectives

The Owingses' investment objectives are similar to those of all imminent retirees—and all retirees for that matter. They want to accomplish two things with their investments from here on out:

1. To provide sufficient income from their investments, which, when combined with Social Security retirement benefits, pension plans, and other sources of

retirement income, are sufficient to meet immediate needs.

2. To provide enough income throughout retirement to avoid the possibility of having to reduce living expenses in old age or, worse, exhausting resources.

The reason why the Owingses are so perplexed by the conflicting opinions about investing retirement resources is that the objectives themselves conflict. Retirees need both income and growth to meet their near- and long-term financial objectives. To further complicate matters, growth, which is essential to meet rising future income needs, should be achieved without unduly risking capital. This is a delicate balancing act. And although much of the advice that the Owingses have been receiving makes sense, each recommendation tends to emphasize one objective at the expense of the other. For example, putting the money into CDs will preserve current capital and provide income, but will erode future purchasing power. Since the principal value of CDs does not increase, it loses ground to inflation. Investing very aggressively will provide the opportunity for capital growth to meet rising income needs, but may subject a retirement portfolio to an untimely decline in capital if stock or bond prices plummet.

Analysis

Many working-age people harbor the notion that once they retire, they need to make major changes in the way they invest. This is usually not the case, particularly if you have invested wisely and well during your working years. Certainly, the investment time horizon for a new retiree has not suddenly diminished, as some would suggest. Your life expectancy on your first day of retirement is only one day less than it was on your last day of work. Retirees are still long-term investors. True, the investment portfolio will need to be accessed to help meet living expenses. But, unfortunately, many retirees tend to let the real need for income and the perceived need for safety dictate wholesale—and usually imprudent— changes in investment selection and strategy.

This is not to say that retirees should make no changes in the way they invest. But any changes made should usually be to fine-tune their investment portfolios. It all depends, of course, on how retirees invest prior to retirement. In the Owingses' case, since they've invested well during their working years, the need for change is truly one of fine-tuning—to reduce risk somewhat and to increase current income.

Allocation of Investment Portfolio

As Table 19-2 indicates, the Owingses have an allocation of 60 percent stocks and 40 percent bonds. (While they also maintain some cash reserves, these have been omitted from this analysis.) This is an overall allocation that the Owingses are comfortable with and is reasonable for a couple in their early sixties. Therefore, no change in their overall investment allocation should be necessary at this point.

Fine-tuning the Portfolio

While the Owingses' overall investment allocation is satisfactory, as Table 19-2 reveals, the categories in which their stocks and stock funds are invested are perhaps too aggressive as they approach retirement. With respect to bonds (all of their bond money is in bond funds), the emphasis has been on municipals because of the Owingses' high tax bracket.

As the table illustrates, the Owingses should reallocate their stocks and stock funds to reduce risk somewhat and provide for additional current income, which they will need to help meet living expenses. Exposure to the high-risk categories—growth and small-company stocks and stock funds—will be reduced. These resources will be redeployed to lower risk stock categories that still offer growth-potential including growth and income stock funds and international stock funds. Moreover, the greater emphasis on the growth and income stock category will provide the Owingses with higher dividend income to help meet living expenses.

With respect to their bond funds, the Owingses' emphasis on municipal funds has been appropriate in the past because of their high tax bracket. But since their income tax bracket will drop at retirement (this is not the case with many retirees, however), a slight reduction in municipal bond fund investments in favor of government bond funds seems appropriate. Since they will soon be in a lower tax bracket, the government bond funds will provide a somewhat higher after-tax income than the municipal funds. Another advantage of increasing the emphasis on government bonds is that this will reduce somewhat the overall risk in their bond portfolio, which, up to this point, had been largely invested in single-state municipal bond funds.

Not unlike many individuals and couples approaching retirement, the Owingses have been perplexed by conflicting guidance on how to invest their money once retirement commences. But the prudent course of action for them—as is often the case with preretirees and recent retirees—is not one of making substantial changes in the way they invest. Instead, fine-tuning their investments to reduce risk and increase income, while still providing for needed growth of capital, will help them achieve a financially comfortable retirement, both now and for the rest of their lives.

―――――――――――― **Table 19-2** ――――――――――――

Fine-Tuning a Retirement Portfolio

	CURRENT	FINE TUNED
STOCKS AND STOCK FUNDS		
Growth	30%	20%
Growth and income	15	25
Small company	10	5
International	5	10
Subtotal stock funds	60%	60%
BOND FUNDS		
Corporate	10	10
Government	5	15
Municipal	25	15
Subtotal bond funds	40%	40%
Total	100%	100%

Who Are You Investing For?

The investment allocation formulas that appear in Chapter 1 are based on age, and the older you get, the more conservative (in investing, if not in politics) you get. But, if you're retired, who are you investing for? Many affluent retirees may well be investing not only for themselves, but also for their children, grandchildren, nieces, or nephews. If so, the way a retiree should invest may be quite different from the way the formulas suggest. Consider the following case study:

CASE STUDY:
A Multigenerational Investment Portfolio for Seniors

Background

Joan and David Smith are a retired couple in their early seventies. They have two adult children and four grandchildren, their own mortgage-free home, and a sizable investment portfolio—about $1 million, and that is in addition to their pensions and Social Security. Thanks to their earlier successful careers and wise financial management, they are now enjoying a well-deserved retirement with a great sense of financial security.

Investing has always been an important part of their financial lives. Recently, they have been thinking about their investment goals, and have come to the conclusion that they may not be investing their money as wisely as they had thought. So they are in the process of revising their investment allocation so that it will better meet not only their immediate needs, but also their long-term financial goals.

Analysis

For many, retirement is a time of financial, as well as social freedom. Indeed, older people have options that are not available to younger people: Their children are (hopefully) no longer dependent on the family dole, their mortgages are paid off, and they have accumulated sufficient financial assets to be both able to keep up with inflation and not to fear running out of money for the rest of their lives. Joan and David are among this group. They are in a position to be aggressive with their investments, certainly beyond money market funds and CDs. The question they now raise, however, is whether they're being aggressive enough.

A simple question that Joan recently asked David precipitated this reevaluation. "Who are we investing our money for? Us—or the children and grandchildren?" The answer was both groups—three generations—but they seemed to be investing the money as if it were all going to be used by the elder family members. As David noted, "Our portfolio does pay attention to growth, but it is really an old folks portfolio with utility stocks, income funds, and a lot of bonds and bond funds. If any of the kids were investing like that, I'd tell them to pay more attention to growth. Invest in areas that will pay off over the next twenty or thirty years when you'll need the money."

Joan and David have long wanted to leave something to their children and grandchildren, just like many other parents and grandparents. They estimate that they will easily be able to pass on $400,000 of their current $1,000,000 to their children and grandchildren. So, after some brief introspection, they have concluded that they should carve out this portion of their assets to invest more aggressively for long-term growth.

Investment Strategy

Joan and David have made the following investment decisions. First, they have divided their total assets into two portfolios, with portfolio A of $600,000 for themselves (all of their retirement plan assets are included in this portfolio) and portfolio B of $400,000 that will eventually go to the children and grandchildren. Portfolio A includes both growth and income investments, and portfolio B heavily emphasizes growth.

Portfolio A

For the "patriarch's and matriarch's" portfolio, they will invest 50 percent in bonds and bond funds, 40 percent in dividend-paying stocks, growth and income funds, and equity income funds, and the remaining 10 percent in growth stocks and growth mutual funds.

Bonds and bond funds

They are diversifying their bond investments with corporate bond funds (for their retirement accounts), U.S. Treasury funds, and municipal bond funds. Within each, they are laddering maturities with short-, intermediate-, and long-term bonds and bond funds.

Dividend-paying stocks, growth and income funds, and equity income funds

Joan and David particularly like dividend-paying stocks, especially those that invest in companies with solid records of raising their dividends and growth and income funds. In addition to paying generous dividends, these funds historically have provided capital appreciation that has kept their money ahead of inflation.

Growth stocks and growth funds

With 90 percent of the portfolio invested in bonds and relatively conservative stocks, Joan and David are now happy to take some risk by investing the remaining 10 percent in growth stocks and growth funds.

Portfolio B

Portfolio B is being set up for the children and grandchildren. Joan and David are going to invest all of this money in mutual funds so they won't have to spend too much time managing the portfolio. The overall investment allocation is 40 percent aggressive growth funds, 30 percent small cap funds, and 30 percent international funds. "Admittedly, this is very aggressive, but the kids aren't going to touch this money for another twenty years. And, when this portfolio is considered in conjunction with Joan's and my portfolio, the overall allocation isn't wildly out of line. Long-term, we're still very bullish."

Aggressive growth funds

They have 40 percent of the assets invested in aggressive growth funds. With time on their side, the eventual shareholders—Joan and David's children and grandchildren—will be able to handle the market volatility inherent in aggressive growth funds. They may also add some sector funds to this category.

Small-cap stock funds

They understand that these funds, while striving for maximum capital gains by investing in companies in developing industries, or small but fast-moving companies, can be very volatile in the short term, but in the long run, they tend to outperform the larger-cap funds and deliver excellent returns to their shareholders.

International funds

They have invested another 30 percent of the kids' and grandkids' portfolio in international stock funds. Again, for long-term, growth-oriented portfolios, international stocks—including international funds that invest in large-cap, small-cap, and emerging markets stocks—offer attractive potential. International funds also offer additional diversification, which is particularly desirable for an aggressive portfolio.

Joan and David are quite satisfied with their "new look" portfolios. They understand though, that they need to review periodically, and if necessary rebalance their portfolios, depending upon their changing financial needs and changed market conditions.

Table 19-3

Portfolio A

THE "PATRIARCH'S AND MATRIARCH'S" PORTFOLIO

Bonds and bond funds	50%
Growth and income stocks and stock funds	40
Growth stocks and stock funds	10
	100%

Table 19-4

Portfolio B

THE CHILDREN'S AND GRANDCHILDREN'S PORTFOLIO

Aggressive growth funds	40%
Small-company funds	30
International stock funds	30
	100%

Still Not Convinced You Should Invest for Growth?

If you need a little more convincing of how important it is to invest for growth when you're retired, consider the following pyramid chart, which shows the number of years money will last at a given withdrawal rate. To illustrate how the chart works, consider two different investors, both age sixty-five.

Sam Savings Account likes to keep his money safe so he puts all of his retirement stash in a bank savings account that pays 3 percent interest. Beverly Bluechip, on the other hand, likes dividend-paying stocks as well as some bonds. She is pretty confident that she can earn at least 7 percent on her money. Both Sam and Bev figure that they could need to live off their money for the next thirty years. Here's the test: At what percentage rate could Sam and Beverly withdraw their money so they could be pretty confident that it will last for thirty years?

The answers will show you how important investing for growth can be. The pyramid chart shows that Sam Savings Account can withdraw 5 percent of his money that earns just 3 percent each year and have it last thirty years. Beverly, on the other hand, can withdraw 8 percent of her money each year, based on her as-

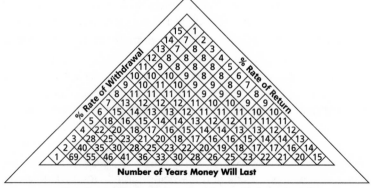

How long will money last at a given withdrawal rate?

sumed 7 percent annual rate of return. That's a lot more than Sam can withdraw. If they each have $300,000, Sam could withdraw $15,000 ($300,000 × 5%), but Beverly can withdraw $24,000 ($300,000 × 8%). That's $175 more per week!

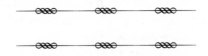

Avoiding Investment Scams

While everyone who has any money at all is a luscious target for a scam artist, some people are more attractive than others. The older you are, the greater the likelihood that someone out there is going to test your financial mettle. Retirees, especially widows, are a preferred target.

Victims of investment scams almost always suffer from the dual afflictions of greed and ignorance. It was the Greek philosopher, Socrates, who affirmed that a knowledgeable person is distinguished by knowing what he or she doesn't know. In financial matters, this should be your philosophical maxim: Know what you don't know. Greed may be the more difficult impediment to overcome, because there is an element of greed in investing. After all, a higher return is better than a lower return. But when someone offers you an investment that promises stellar returns, remember that high return means high risk. In the hands of the scam artist— or even the unscrupulous broker—a promise of high returns is simply an attempt to appeal to your greed.

The fraud operators and investment opportunists are very good at their craft, but believe me, bunk is bunk, no matter how pretty the wrapping or flowery the words. In fact, the prettier the wrapping and the more flowery the words, the greater the likelihood that you're being duped. So if it sounds too good to be true, it probably is. If it sounds too simple to be believed, it is probably very complex. If you think you are being misled, you probably are. And if you find you are being pressured, you most likely are being pressured. Words alone won't suffice. The scam artist knows how to tell a tall tale and make it sound persuasive.

How do you avoid being taken? Here are a couple of guidelines:

• **Never buy on impulse, especially from a complete stranger.** The likelihood of disaster, no matter how safe it seems, is guaranteed to be titanic. Be especially careful of boiler room operators who will try to sell you virtually any investment. Often it is an investment that plays on people's fears and greed. It is simply unbelievable how many people get taken over the telephone. If you are ever tempted to send in your money over the telephone, do the following. First, request information in writing. Of course, they'll tell you that you must act now, but be firm. Chances are the information will never arrive, but if it does, you can examine it without the sales pitch.

• **Always get a second opinion from a relative or friend.** You get a second opinion before having surgery—you should also get a second opinion before somebody removes a good portion of your investment account. Here's a rule that I urge senior citizens to follow: Always double-check any commitment of money for any reason. Ask a trusted friend, accountant, or lawyer—even your children or other relatives—before you plunk down a large chunk of cash. (I consider a large chunk to be anything over $500.)

——∞∞∞——

A Short Course on Investing

If you are new to investing, please read this section to learn some basics. Investing isn't that complicated. If you can arm yourself with some basic investing knowledge, you will be able to make your own investment decisions. You can be your own investment adviser, because investing isn't as complicated as most people think. It does take some effort to educate yourself about how to manage your money, but once you know the basics, it's really not that difficult. If you decide to use someone to advise you on investing, still read this section because the more you understand about investing, the better you will be able to work with your adviser.

What Do You Want Your Money to Do for You?

The first step is to determine what goals you have for your money. Accumulating enough money to be able to retire comfortably is certainly a goal for all working-age people. Everyone should be concerned with retirement. Many people who are young and see retirement as a long way off may not be thinking about retirement, but you should be. There are also other common goals besides retirement that people have for investing their money. You may have a goal for something more immediate, such as buying a car or taking a vacation. Saving for a house or saving for college for the kids are other common goals. Retired people are concerned about having enough income to live comfortably and to be able to keep up with inflation.

Take a moment now to summarize the financial goals you have in the following list.

My financial goals:
1. _____
2. _____
3. _____
4. _____
5. _____

When Do You Want to Achieve Your Goals?

Now that you've determined your financial goals, you next need to decide how soon you want to reach each one of them. If you plan to need money for a goal within three years—to buy a car for example—consider that a short-term goal. A long-term goal is eight or more years. Consider anything in between as a medium-term goal. Because, as we'll see later, the time when you need your money to meet your goals will be very important for making your investment choices.

Typically, we have goals in all three of these areas—short-term, medium-term, and long-term. All of us are at different stages of our lives and so our goals are different. Therefore, our strategies for investing will often need to change as we move through life.

One of the most important factors in deciding where to

invest your money is how soon you are going to need it. For short-term goals, safety is the most important factor; with money you'll be spending soon you don't want the value of your money to drop just before you need it. For long-term goals, growth is important; your money needs to increase in value enough to stay ahead of inflation. Deciding how much of each you need—how much safety and how much growth— is one of the most important parts of deciding how to invest your money.

There is a third factor that is important to many people: income. Just as you earn a paycheck, your investments can earn money for you that can be spent on day-to-day expenses or reinvested. Deciding where to put your money means thinking about those three things: safety, growth, and income. When you expect to need a certain part of your savings in just two or three years, you need to keep that money safe. You don't want the value of those savings to go up and down a lot. On the other hand, when your investment goals are long term, say over eight years away, then you want to focus on growth. Medium-term goals are less clear-cut. You may want some combination. Perhaps you'd want some growth to help build your savings and some income to help balance out the ups and downs of investing for growth.

Three Investor Profiles

We need to discuss further how growth, income, and safety fit into your investing strategy. To help with this, let me introduce three typical hypothetical situations. Each of these profiles is summarized below.

Profile 1: Darrell

Darrell is twenty-five years old, single, and just starting out in life.

Age: Twenty-five
Status: Single
Income: $20,000
Financial goals: New car, vacation

Profile 2: Sally

Sally, who is forty, is a single mother with two kids, aged fourteen and sixteen.

Age: Forty
Status: Single; two children, ages fourteen and sixteen
Income: $37,000
Financial goals: College tuition for two sons; saving for retirement; replacing worn-out car

Profile 3: Betty and Joe

Betty and Joe are empty nesters who are about three years away from retirement.

Ages: Close to retirement
Status: Married
Income: $52,000
Financial goal: Retirement

Each of these people has a different set of needs for their money, is at a different stage of their lives, and each needs to use a different approach to investing.

Let's start with **Darrell.** Darrell believes that his biggest concern is income. He wants to make a lot of money now, maybe to buy a new car or take some nice vacations. He is like a lot of people his age, he is looking pretty much at short-term goals.

But let's take a look at his investment future. He may want to buy a house in a few years. If so, that would be a medium-term goal. And assuming he might want to get married and have kids, he should include college tuition as a long-term goal now. Also, retirement is clearly a long-term goal as well. Now Darrell, at twenty-five, probably isn't thinking very much about retirement, but he should be. He has a long time for his money to grow for retirement if he starts saving for it now. Even if it's just a small amount to start, savings can make a big difference in how much he has when he retires.

Now let's look at **Sally.** She is thinking right now primarily about sending her kids to college. She also knows that she needs to save for her retirement. At her age, of course, she needs to think of growth for her retirement goals since it's a long time off. College is another situation. She will probably need a combination of growth and income for her medium-term goal of getting the kids through college. She also has some short-term goals, in other words, goals that need to be paid for within three years. One of her kids will be entering college in a couple of years, and she needs to replace her car soon. She'll need to set aside some money for those things in a safe place.

Since Sally is a single parent, you may think she should be pretty conservative with her money. She certainly does need to be conservative for part of it, but she can't emphasize safety for all of her money because, for her long-term goals, she'll lose ground to inflation unless she is focusing on growth.

Finally, let's look at **Betty and Joe.** Betty and Joe are three years from retirement and are worried about safety—protecting their nest egg. They know they are going to need to live off their investments when they retire, so they don't want to take any risks with it. For Betty and Joe, retirement seems like a short-term goal. But think about it. What happens if they live into their nineties—that's another thirty years! For Betty and Joe retirement fits into short-term, medium-term, *and* long-term goals. So even if you are very close to retirement, you still need to consider it as a long-term goal as well as a short-term goal, because you are likely to need that money to last for a long time. Retirees need to invest for both income (to meet their living expenses) and growth (so that they can keep up with ever-rising living costs later in life).

Now that you understand a bit more about your investment time horizon, go back to the goals you listed on page 205, and indicate next to each whether it is a short-term, medium-term, or long-term goal. Remember that in some instances, for example a child about to enter college or if you're about to retire, a particular goal may cover more than one period.

Risk Is Not a Four-Letter Word

No one wants to risk losing money, especially losing money on investments. But there are two kinds of risk: the kind you can see and the kind you can't. The kind you can't see is the risk that comes from inflation and what it means to the buying power of your income. Let me give you an example. At a 3½ percent inflation rate per year, your cost of living doubles every twenty years. It could go higher than that. So for every $20 you spend today, you'll need $40 in twenty years, and double that again for the next twenty years. In forty years, for the $20 you need today, you'll need $80.

So let's consider someone at age twenty-five whose living expenses are $25,000 today. When he is forty-five, he'll be spending over $50,000 for the same expenses if inflation averages 3½ percent per year. When he retires in another twenty years, he will need $100,000—or maybe $80,000 if he can live on 20 percent less in his retirement.

Here's another example that looks at inflation a little differently. It shows how inflation affects purchasing power. Someone who is planning for retirement figures that, in addition to Social Security, he'll need $25,000 in income for living expenses when he retires. Now $25,000 happens to be just what his retirement income is expected to be. So he thinks he's in good shape. But consider how inflation can affect the purchasing power of his $25,000 over his retirement years. If inflation is 3½ percent per year, after less than seven years our retiree has seen his purchasing power drop to $20,000. After twenty years, his purchasing power can be cut in half. So that $25,000 of income, which looked so good at retirement, could be worth far less in terms of purchasing power later in life.

These numbers are pretty scary, I admit. But they show how much risk is involved in just letting your money sit and not grow enough to outpace inflation. Some fear investing because they can see the stock market go up and down and interest rates go up and down. That's the kind of risk you can see. So they think they can put their money somewhere where it will be safe, but that pays low interest. If you don't take into account what you can't see from inflation, you will really be missing the boat. Table A-1 compares inflation risk with investment risk.

Table A-1

Inflation Risk vs. Investment Risk

THE INVISIBLE RISK OF INFLATION	VISIBLE RISK FROM INVESTMENTS
• means your money loses buying power over time	• means the value of your initial investment could go up or down
• is caused by increases over time in the cost of living	• is caused by different factors that depend on the type of investment
• is less of a potential problem in the short-term	• is historically less of a problem over the long-term
• can be managed by investing to try to get a rate of return that is higher than or keeps pace with inflation	• can be managed by deciding how much and what kind of investment risk to take, and how much to diversify
• is associated mostly with short-term investments.	• is associated mostly with stocks and bonds.

Now you may conclude that there is a risk in everything. And there is, but you can minimize the risk that you can see—the visible risk from investments. Inflation is an invisible risk—you can't see it and you have no control over it and everyone has to deal with it. You actually have more control over visible risk—that is the kind you have when you invest in stocks and bonds—because you can control how much and what kind of risk you take. There are several ways to reduce your amount of visible risk.

The Three Main Types of Investment Tools

As we have seen, one of the most important factors in deciding where to put your money is how soon you'll need it. Do you need your money to grow? Do you need it to produce income? Do you need it to stay safe?

There are three main types of investments, each geared mostly toward one of the three key things you need from your money: growth, income, and safety. I say mostly, because an investment behaves very differently over the short term—say two to three years—than it does over the long term, say eight years or more. The same investments can behave very differently over different periods.

Short-term investments

There are three basic kinds of investments: short-term investments, bonds, and stocks. Let's discuss short-term investments first, since they are the most familiar. The short-term investments that most of us know are short-term CDs, bank savings accounts, money market funds, and U.S. Treasury bills. In essence, short-term investments maintain a relatively stable value, pay interest, and can be easily changed into cash. Of the three types of investments, short-term investments pay the lowest rate of return. So why invest in them at all? Well, people buy these primarily for safety. You do get some income from them, but what's most important is their stability. When you go into a short-term investment, you can be pretty sure about how much money you'll get out of it. You are not taking much visible risk of losing money on your investment. The prices of these types of investments don't go up and down the way that other investments do.

So when would a short-term investment be a good investment? Well, if you are going to buy something in the next year or two, it's good to know the money will be there when you need it. On the other hand, if you're not going to need the money within a few years, you may not want to keep that money in a short-term investment, because you're facing much more invisible risk from inflation. Remember how inflation cuts your buying power over time? That's the danger with short-term investments. In effect, you are losing money—losing purchasing power—without even realizing it.

Bonds

Bonds are like IOUs. When you lend somebody money, you get an IOU from the borrower. (Of course, if you lend money to your child and get an IOU, good luck trying to get the money back.) A bond is like an IOU. You lend money to a corporation or a government agency in return for receiving regular payments of interest on the loan you made as well as the repayment of principal when the loan matures. That interest provides income. That's the most important reason people buy bonds. That income can help them pay their bills, or it can be reinvested. The income can also help even out the ups and downs that both bond and stock prices go through. Bonds usually pay more interest than short-term investments, but like stocks, their prices can change. Bond prices and interest rates are like the opposite ends of a seesaw. When interest rates decline, bond prices rise. But when interest rates rise, bond prices will likely decline. That means that if you have money in bonds, the overall value of that investment could go down even though you are receiving interest income. Bond interest rates stay fixed until the bond matures—that's why they are often called "fixed-income investments." But their prices go up and down depending on what interest rates in general do. The longer the bond's maturity—that is the longer until the loan will be repaid in full—the more the price can go up and down.

Stocks

When you own a share of stock, you own a share of a company. How much of the company you own depends on the number of shares you have. Stocks are sometimes called "equities" because they are like the equity in your house. You own a part of something—in this case, the company. With your house, the bank has the rest of your equity. With stock, the other stockholders share the equity in the company. People invest in stocks primarily for growth. As a group, stocks go up and down in value more than any other type of investment over the short term. But over time, stocks have been one of the few types of investments that have beaten inflation. There's no guarantee that what has happened in the past will continue in the future, of course, but the average yearly return on stocks has been a little over 10 percent. Historically, stocks have grown much faster than bonds and short-term investments. People are often afraid of stocks because they hear about bear markets or stock market crashes. And that should be a concern to investors who will need the money within just a few years. But over the long run, there is more risk of losing money to inflation if you don't invest in stocks. Yes, the visible risk of stocks periodically losing value is higher in the short term than other investments, but with proper investment allocation (described in Chapters 1 and 2), you can protect yourself from those risks *and* from loss from inflation.

Mutual funds

Many people think mutual funds are a fourth kind of investment in addition to short-term investments, bonds, and stocks. They are actually not. Mutual funds are a way to put money into the three types of investments that were discussed above. Mutual funds are a way that individuals can help protect themselves against the risks of investing in just one company or with one lender. They allow you to pool your money with other investors. Then the fund manager buys one of the three types of investments to concentrate on and picks many different stocks, or many different bonds, or many different short-term investments, or some funds that invest in both stocks and bonds, etc.

Each fund has its own way of trying to make money, called its "investment objective." Based on those guidelines, a professional manager decides which stocks and/or bonds to buy.

Stock mutual funds and bond mutual funds are pretty much self-explanatory. As I mentioned, some funds invest in both stocks and bonds—balanced mutual funds for example. A money market fund is a mutual fund that buys short-term investments.

One other investment term that is important to understand is *total return*. Total return includes not only income earned from an investment through interest or dividends, but also any increase or decrease in the price of the investment. For example, if you get 6 percent interest on a bond, but the price of the bond drops 10 percent, your total return is −4 percent. On the other hand, if you get 6 percent interest on a bond and its price rises by 8 percent, your total return is +14 percent. Total return, rather than the interest or the dividend that an investment pays, is the best way to compare different types of investments and to evaluate how your investments have performed.

Managing Investment Risk

Now that you understand the various kinds of investments, it's time to look at managing the risk that each poses. The best way to manage risk is to put time on your side. Investing for long periods means you have a long time to ride out the ups and downs experienced by the stock market. As I said earlier, stocks can go up and down in the short term, but the historical trend over time has been up.

Second, avoid putting all your eggs in one basket. When you diversify by investing in many different stocks or bonds instead of just one, you reduce the impact of any one stock's or any one bond's eroding on your money. You're spreading around your risk. One way you can do this is with mutual funds.

Third, you can reduce your risk even further by investing in all three types of investments: stocks, bonds, and short-term investments. The fancy term for this is *asset allocation* or *investment allocation,* which really means nothing more than how you divvy up your savings among the three types of investments. My four easy steps to successful investing, discussed in Chapters 1–4, are built around allocating your investments.

Combining the types of investments you make can help minimize risks because if one type is doing badly, another may be doing quite well. That way, you don't have to do everything right, you just have to do more right than wrong. If everything is in one basket, you have only one chance to get it right. While investment allocation does not guarantee against a loss, it can help you minimize both the visible risk—that investments and stocks and bonds will periodically decline in value—and the invisible risk of inflation. Remember, stocks are generally for growth, bonds are generally for income, and short-term investments are generally for short-term safety to meet financial needs that you will have in the near future. Allocating your investments properly by putting your eggs in a variety of baskets is the best way to minimize both kinds of risk.

Finally, the way you divide up your investments is up to your own circumstances and judgment, but it is terribly important to your long-term investment success. So devote some time to thinking about the best way to divvy up your investments. It will be time well spent.

APPENDIX B

How to Purchase Investments

The multitrillion-dollar financial services industry continues to boom. Competition abounds, and where there is a lot of competition, informed investors can benefit mightily. If you're a little unsure about how to purchase investments, let me help. With so many different kinds of investments from which to choose, so many firms at your service—not to mention scores of discount brokers and thousands of low- and no-commission mutual funds—and an ever-changing market, the process of purchasing investments often lives up to its reputation of being a financial jungle. There are many ways to get through the jungle without coming down with jungle fever, however.

The mechanics of purchasing investments are less complicated than most people think. In fact, purchasing investments is, in many instances, only a matter of picking up a phone and placing your order.

Opening a Mutual Fund Account

If you want to invest in mutual funds exclusively, the simplest way to go about it is to open up an account with one or more of the mutual fund companies. The phone call is free (the big mutual fund companies advertise in the financial pages of the newspaper. You can get their numbers there, or call 800 information at 1-800-555-1212). When you call a fund company, the cheerful person at the other end of the line will be more than happy to send you the application materials. Or, if you want advice on selecting mutual funds, you can open up a full-service brokerage account which is described below.

Finally, if you want to invest in mutual funds from a variety of fund families, which makes a lot of sense to me, then the best route may be to open up an account at one of the large discount brokers who offer "mutual fund buying services." These services allow you to buy mutual funds from many different fund families at either no fee or a very low fee. See The Best of All Worlds below.

In addition to transacting business over the phone, many larger mutual fund companies also have investor service centers in large cities where you can open up your account and make trades. Similar to full service brokers and discount brokers, mutual fund companies offer a variety of bells and whistles, including check-writing privileges, automatic investment programs, and sweep accounts that make sure all of your money is working for you rather than sitting idle in a noninterest-bearing account.

Opening a Brokerage Account

Purchasing individual stocks requires that you set up a brokerage account. It's often easier to open up a brokerage account than it is to open up a checking account at your local bank. (If you want, you can do both at the same time since many banks offer their customers the option of buying stocks, bonds, short-term investments and mutual funds through a brokerage account established at the bank.) However, just because the mechanics of opening up a brokerage account are easy doesn't mean the task of selecting a suitable firm to meet your investment needs is.

First decide what you want your brokerage account to accomplish for you. Whether you are planning to be an active, semiactive, or hands-off investor will directly affect the type of account you will select. Second, you need to outline your investment plan after reading the first sections of this book and detail how you will go about putting your plan into action. Finally, you need to decide how much and what kind of investment advice you need. Will you be making most or all of the investment decisions yourself? There are three levels of brokerage services available to you. The type of account (or accounts) you open depends on how you responded to the points raised above.

Full-service broker

A full-service broker provides customers with research and recommendations. Full-service brokers have research departments with analysts at the ready to support any recommendation or deliver an advisory answer to your question. If you're new to the market—haven't a clue about the most basic investment techniques and maneuvers—you might decide to go to a full-service broker. Moreover, many experienced investors prefer to deal with full-service brokers as well. But always keep in mind that since full-service brokers are paid on commission, they may be motivated to transact more business in your account than you need.

Discount brokers

With a discount broker, you call all the investment shots. You are responsible for initiating the buy-and-sell orders. The commissions you pay are considerably less than the commission you'd pay to a full-service broker since there is no individual broker involved. The result is a less costly way to invest.

So with more than a little (but less than a lot of) legwork, you can buy your own stocks and bonds through a discount broker. In order to distinguish themselves from other discount brokers and "deep discount" brokers (discussed below), some discount brokerage firms are offering limited assistance to investors. This may come either in the form of stock and industry research reports and/or the opportunity to speak with a broker who can offer limited assistance.

Deep discount brokers

Finally, deep discount brokers offer rock-bottom commissions in exchange for—nothing. Deep discounters are designed for active traders who require no guidance. If you are an active investor who absolutely, positively makes your own investment decisions, then there is no question; a deep discount broker is the most cost-effective way to go.

If you go either the discount or deep-discount route, you may well want to reduce your trading costs even more by trading on-line with your computer. (See pages 115–117.)

Which way to go? It may not be an either/or decision

Nothing in your financial life is either/or, although there may be some in the financial services industry who would like you to believe otherwise. Many experienced and active investors find that they invest most effectively with both a full-service and a discount or deep-discount brokerage account. The discounter can be used when making transactions that you initiate, and the full-service broker can be used to obtain research and recommendations and to buy investments based upon the firm and broker's research and recommendations.

Other Great Ways to Purchase Investments

Investment clubs

An investment club is a group of investment-minded people who pool their resources to invest on a regular basis, and who meet regularly to review and revise their investments and investment strategies. Investment clubs can be a great way to learn more about investing in individual stocks. For more information, see page 103.

Dividend reinvestment plans

If you have already purchased stock in a corporation, and if you expect the company stock to do well, then dividend reinvestment is one of the smartest ways to purchase new shares in the company. Why? Because corporations will purchase the shares for you either through the automatic reinvestment of your dividends or if you send in more money by purchasing additional shares of their stock. The icing on the cake is that they'll allow you to purchase and sell these shares at either no commission or at a sharply reduced commission. Some companies even offer these shares to you at a slight discount.

In order to participate in these dividend reinvestment and optional purchase plans, you must first buy at least one share of stock through a broker. A growing number of companies, however, are allowing investors to buy their first shares directly from the company at no commission. This means you can buy stock without paying any brokerage commissions!

Stock purchase plans

If you work for a company whose stock is traded on the stock exchange, you may have the opportunity to participate in a stock purchase plan. Stock purchase plans offer employees convenience and often discounts in the purchase price of their company's stock. They provide employees a stake in the present and future of the company—a novel approach to pride and profitability. It's a route to stock ownership well worth considering—if it's available and if you are confident of your company's future success. If the company offers you stock at a discount—a 15 percent discount is typical—you're throwing money away if you don't participate. But remember not to put too many eggs in one basket. In general, if more than 20 percent of your investments are tied up in the stock of a single company, that's too much. Nevertheless, you still may want to participate in the stock purchase plan if a discount is available. You can always sell the stock (usually at little or no commission) right after the stock purchase plan has bought the shares for you. If the shares were purchased at a discount, you make an immediate profit.

The Best of All Worlds

If you make all or most of your investment decisions yourself and you like to invest both in mutual funds and directly owned stocks and bonds, you can get the best of both worlds by opening up a discount brokerage account that also has a mutual fund buying service. While Charles Schwab & Co., Fidelity Investments, and Jack White & Company are the pioneers, other discounters are offering these great accounts as well. They allow you to combine your stocks, bonds, *and* your mutual funds in one account. The discounter offers a wide range of no-load mutual funds from numerous fund families that can be purchased through their mutual fund buying service. Many funds are available at absolutely no cost. Others require a small fee for buying and selling the fund, but this is a small price to pay for the wonderful convenience that these accounts offer.

Important Decisions When Opening Up an Account

You will have to make some seemingly innocuous decisions when you open up an investment account. Nevertheless, you should exercise care when making these decisions.

Single or Joint Account?

A single account is registered in your name and your name only. A joint account, on the other hand, is in the name of two or more people. For many couples, a joint account may be the preferred choice. It allows either partner to authorize purchases and sales. On the other hand, holding investments in joint name—whether with a spouse, partner, or other family member—can cause some big estate problems when one of the account holders dies. Therefore, I think you should speak with the attorney who has drawn up your will to see whether or not putting any investment account in joint name is okay.

Cash or Margin Account?

A cash account is usually the small investor's best choice. A cash account simply means that all your transactions must be paid in cash—either through money market funds available in your account or through an additional payment of cash by you. In this age of too much debt, paying cash is a sensible way to build your investment portfolio.

In contrast to a cash account, margin accounts enable an investor to buy "on margin." Investing on margin is like taking out a loan to place a bet. In this case, you take a loan—usually no more than 50 percent of the money in your brokerage account—to purchase investments. It's a risky way to invest, and you are charged interest (prime rate plus 1 to 3 percent) for the privilege. Investors who really get clobbered in declining markets are those who invest on margin. As the value of their investments declines, they are required to put up more money to cover their margin loans. If they don't have the money, they are forced to sell some of their investments at a most inopportune time.

Nondiscretionary or discretionary account?

A nondiscretionary account requires the broker to obtain your approval prior to making any purchases or sales in your account. A discretionary account allows your broker to invest your money at his or her discretion without getting your authority to do so. I wouldn't opt for a discretionary account unless and until you have a lot of experience with and confidence in your broker. Early on in the relationship, it's important to have your broker review his or her ideas with you. It's one more way you can learn about investing. If you eventually decide on a discretionary account, it becomes doubly important to review carefully each and every transaction report (you should receive one of these every time there is transaction in your account) and the monthly statements. Why? Brokers have been known to change from Dr. Jekyll to Mr. Hyde after the customer has authorized a discretionary account.

**Send for Information on Jonathan's Latest
List of All-Star Mutual Funds**

To receive information on how to order the latest list of over
eighty all-star mutual funds in all mutual fund categories, send
a self-addressed stamped envelope to:

Four Steps
P.O. Box 350
Watertown, MA 02272

The list is updated quarterly, so you'll receive an up-to-date
list of outstanding funds, including toll-free phone numbers
to order prospectuses.

ACKNOWLEDGMENTS

This book has benefited immensely from the assistance of several people, particularly Lisa Considine and Tom Colgan, my editors at Avon Books, and Pauline Kelly. Also, special thanks to the many people I've had the pleasure of speaking with over the past several years—on the talk shows and during personal appearances. Your questions and suggestions have been extremely useful in putting together this book—one that I hope will help all individual investors achieve their financial dreams. Thank you.

INDEX

———∞∞∞———